Praise for
Human Resource Development Research Handbook

"If research is the seed, this book is the tool to till the soil."

—Kendrick B. Melrose, Chairman and CEO, The Toro Company,
and author of *Making the Grass Greener on Your Side*

"Finally, a book that brings research out of the ivory tower and into the hands of HRD practitioners."

—Gary R. Sisson, President, Paradigm Corporation

"Corporate leaders should be very interested in the avenues to excellence covered in this handbook."

—Timothy McClernon, Senior Vice President, Piper Jaffray Companies

---

"The *Human Resource Development Research Handbook* is unique—it speaks clearly to both seasoned and beginning scholars."

—Irwin L. Goldstein, Professor and Dean, University of Maryland

---

"The American Society for Training and Development and the Academy of Human Resource Development are strongly committed to advancing the theory and practice of HRD. This book is a big step toward that goal."

—Laurie J. Bassi, Vice President of Research, American Society
for Training and Development

Berrett-Koehler Publishers

BERRETT-KOEHLER is an independent publisher of books, periodicals, and other publications at the leading edge of new thinking and innovative practice on work, business, management, leadership, stewardship, career development, human resources, entrepreneurship, and global sustainability.

Since the company's founding in 1992, we have been committed to supporting the movement toward a more enlightened world of work by publishing books, periodicals, and other publications that help us to integrate our values with our work and work lives, and to create more humane and effective organizations.

We have chosen to focus on the areas of work, business, and organizations, because these are central elements in many people's lives today. Furthermore, the work world is going through tumultuous changes, from the decline of job security to the rise of new structures for organizing people and work. We believe that change is needed at all levels—individual, organizational, community, and global—and our publications address each of these levels.

We seek to create new lenses for understanding organizations, to legitimize topics that people care deeply about but that current business orthodoxy censors or considers secondary to bottom-line concerns, and to uncover new meaning, means, and ends for our work and work lives.

Human Resource Development
RESEARCH HANDBOOK

A Publication in
the Berrett-Koehler
Organizational
Performance
Series

Richard A. Swanson &
Barbara L. Swanson
Series Editors

Human Resource Development

RESEARCH HANDBOOK

Linking Research and Practice

Richard A. Swanson
Elwood F. Holton III
Editors

Sponsored by
The Academy of Human Resource Development
&
The American Society for Training and Development

Berrett-Koehler Publishers
San Francisco

Berrett-Koehler Publishers, Inc.
450 Sansome Street, Suite 1200
San Francisco, CA 94111-3320
Tel: (415) 288-0260   Fax: (415) 362-2512

ORDERING INFORMATION

Individual sales. Berrett-Koehler publications are available through most bookstores. They can also be ordered direct from Berrett-Koehler at the address above.

Quantity sales. Special discounts are available on quantity purchases by corporations, associations, and others. For details, contact the "Special Sales Department" at the Berrett-Koehler address above.

Orders for college textbook/course adoption use. Please contact Berrett-Koehler Publishers at the address above.

Orders by U.S. trade bookstores and wholesalers. Please contact Publishers Group West, 4065 Hollis Street, Box 8843, Emeryville, CA 94662. Tel: (510) 658-3453; 1-800-788-3123. Fax: (510) 658-1834.

Printed in the United States of America
Printed on acid-free and recycled paper that is composed of 50% recycled fiber, including 10% postconsumer waste.

Library of Congress Cataloging-in-Publication Data

Human resource development research handbook / Richard A. Swanson,
    Elwood F. Holton III, editors. — 1st ed.
        p.   cm.
    Includes bibliographical references and index.
    ISBN 1-881052-68-0 (alk. paper)
        1. Human capital—Research—Methodology.   I. Swanson, Richard A.,
    1942-   . II. Holton, Ed, 1957-
    HD4904.7.H862   1997
    658.3—dc21   96-53290
                                                                      CIP

First Edition

99 98 97   10 9 8 7 6 5 4 3 2 1

Book Production: Pleasant Run Publishing Services
Composition: Classic Typography

*Dedicated to our children
and the future of all children of the world.*

*Matthew McArthur Baldwin
Kara Ann Burnett
Lauren Elyse Burnett
Tanya DaMommio
Natalie D. Eft
Karen E. Holton
Brian N. McLean
Cynthia L. McLean
Laird D. McLean
Melissa D. McLean
Paul L. McLean
Adam P. Neaman
Jeffrey L. Parker
Katherine E. Parker
Susan C. Parker
Ann F. Passmore
David L. Passmore II
Maureen L. Passmore
Andrew Bruce Sleezer
Robert James Sleezer
Thomas David Sleezer
Christina A. Swanson
R. Eric Swanson
Katherine L. McLean Taylor
Nicholas Reed Torraco
Tyson Watkins
Taylor Winum*

CONTENTS

Foreword: The Seed of Research   ix
   Ken Melrose, *CEO, The Toro Company*

Preface   xiii

Part One: Practical Importance of Research

1. HRD Research: Don't Go to Work Without It!   3
   Richard A. Swanson, *University of Minnesota*

2. How Research Contributes to the HRD Value Chain   21
   Michael P. Leimbach, *Wilson Learning Corporation*
   Timothy T. Baldwin, *Indiana University*

3. HRD Partnerships for Integrating HRD
  Research and Practice   47
   Ronald L. Jacobs, *Ohio State University*

Part Two: Ways of Doing Practical Research

4. Quantitative Research Methods   65
   Elwood F. Holton III, *Louisiana State University*
   Michael F. Burnett, *Louisiana State University*

5. Qualitative Research Methods   88
   Barbara L. Swanson, *Swanson & Associates, Inc.*
   Karen E. Watkins, *University of Georgia*
   Victoria J. Marsick, *Columbia University*

6. Theory-Building Research Methods   114
   Richard J. Torraco, *University of Nebraska*

7. Case Study Research Methods   138
   Victoria J. Marsick, *Columbia University*
   Karen E. Watkins, *University of Georgia*

Part Three: Getting Started on Research

8. Examples of Excellent HRD Research   161
   Gary N. McLean, *University of Minnesota*
   Darlene Russ-Eft, *Zenger Miller*

9. Finding and Using HRD Research   183
   Catherine M. Sleezer, *Oklahoma State University*
   James H. Sleezer, *Data Systems Services*

10. Ways of Seeing: Disciplinary Bases
    of Research in HRD   199
    David L. Passmore, *Pennsylvania State University*

Index   215

The Authors   223

The Seed of Research

Ken Melrose
CEO, *The Toro Company*

In my book *Making the Grass Greener on Your Side*, I tell the story of the rebirth of The Toro Company. As we went through this very productive but painful period of individual and corporate growth, we learned an important lesson. If we were to have sustained long-term growth, we needed to emphasize our strongest corporate asset—our people and their long-term effectiveness. Human resource development became a key focus in our turnaround.

In a similar way, the *Human Resource Development Research Handbook* champions the same emphasis. It is about research, but not the impersonal, ivory-tower type of research. This book is about conducting, using, and partnering for research that truly makes a difference in daily human resource development.

"Get the results any way you can, but get the results" was the motto of Toro's—and many other companies'—culture during the 1970s and 1980s. But when adverse weather and economic cycles put the brakes on Toro's growth, it became evident that only a radical change of culture could pull us out of disaster and give our new direction and momentum greater sustainability through future cycles.

Our challenges forced us to examine thoroughly every aspect of our organization. When we looked for a direction that would lead us back to prosperity, we decided not to go for quick fixes. We decided to "seed, not sod," to grow solutions that would be deep-rooted and able to stand up to the volatility of the marketplace. The seeds we used were our greatest asset: our people.

In cultures that are accustomed to quick results, "seed, not sod" isn't an easy choice. Seeding takes time and a lot of care. When you plant a lawn with seed, you don't see much growth for the first few days and weeks. That's why many people are into sod; they like instant results. Eventually, however, seed develops stronger roots than sod and yields a heathier and stronger turf.

When I first became Toro's president in 1981, the organization, the financial community, and our distributors all wanted a quick fix to our financial situation. Our management did not see any way to do that without sacrificing important, long-term benefits for our people and the company. A new culture was implemented in which employees, customers, and performance were valued, and the results stimulated a long-term positive momentum for quality, productivity, and profits.

This book is about sowing seed, instead of laying sod, in human resource development practice. Ultimately, human resource development, as outlined in this book, will help companies create a seedbed for successful people and foster a tremendous edge over the competition.

The key, as this book points out, is penetrating research, the "seeds" to develop and grow effective employee practices. It is always easy to search for "quick fixes" and instant solutions to "sod" over problem areas in your landscape, especially during crises. But I've seen a people-oriented culture grow at Toro and at other organizations, how it can be a tremendous force to carry a company through tough times, and how it can be an accelerating force for growth when times are easier. Regardless of the times, good or bad, human resource development practices are vital for companies to be competitive in today's global economy.

This handbook represents a significant step forward by making the research process clear and understandable for practitioners. It talks about building partnerships between practitioners and researchers to advance practice and human resource development as a field. It shows practitioners how to use research, and researchers how to work with practitioners. If research is the seed, then this book is the tool to till the soil. Use it and you can expect a more healthy and vibrant professional practice. People-valuing cultures integrate relationships and results. They build stronger people and stronger organizations.

January 1997   Ken Melrose
                                                                CEO
                                                                The Toro Company

PREFACE

Ahhh . . . there is nothing so practical as good research! The fruits of research are principles and theories that, when applied, work time and time again. The *Human Resource Development Research Handbook* grew out of a passion among a group of researchers to help the profession harvest the best from research to improve its theory and practice. One unique aspect of human resource development scholars is their deep commitment to research that informs and improves practice and their belief in sound practice that informs HRD research and theory. Over the years, a number of scholars meeting in various groups talked about the need for a guide to help those practicing in the field to understand research. This research handbook is the product of their vision.

Purpose of This Book

This long-awaited book fills two gaps. One gap is between the demands for practical know-how and sound research—the trusted source of verifiable know-how. The subtitle of this book, "Linking Research and Practice," was taken seriously by the authors. Each contributor has a distinguished HRD career focused on maintaining the integrity of HRD research and HRD practice.

The filling of the second gap represents another milestone in the maturity of HRD as a field of study. Mature fields of study have a scholarly journal: we have the *Human Resource Development Quarterly*. Mature fields of study have a scholarly professional association: we have the *Academy of Human Resource Development*. Mature fields of study have a research handbook: we now have the *Human Resource Development Research Handbook*, which is unique in that it speaks not just to researchers but to practitioners as well.

Overview of the Contents

This handbook is divided in to three parts. In Part One, "Practical Importance of Research," Chapter One builds the practical case for HRD research, Chapter Two focuses on the purposes of research and how research contributes to the value chain, and Chapter Three informs researchers and practitioners of their partnership roles in conducting research.

Part Two of the handbook, "Ways of Doing Practical Research," talks about the conduct of research outside of the ivory tower. Quantitative research methods are covered in Chapter Four and qualitative research methods in Chapter Five. Chapter

Six focuses on theory-building research methods, and case study research methods are discussed in Chapter Seven.

Finally, in Part Three, "Getting Started on Research," Chapter Eight presents examples of nine excellent HRD research studies along with a critique of each. Chapter Nine provides assistance for finding and using HRD research. Chapter Ten, the last chapter of the book, reviews the disciplinary bases of research in HRD and provides inspiration to add to the body of knowledge.

Acknowledgments

This handbook has been nurtured by several groups. Support from the Academy of Human Resource Development Publications Committee and the American Society for Training and Development Research Committee has been critical. Important sources of encouragement came from the growing and increasingly influential community of HRD scholars and from the publisher, Berrett-Koehler.

Many of us believe that sound research should be leading the profession and furthermore that scholars armed with sound research should actively challenge charlatan practices in HRD as well as advance best practices. We welcome you as a potential HRD research partner.

January 1997

Richard A. Swanson
St. Paul, Minnesota

Elwood F. Holton III
Baton Rouge, Louisiana

PART ONE

Practical Importance of Research

HRD Research
Don't Go to Work Without It!

Richard A. Swanson
University of Minnesota

This book is ultimately about the expertise required to get consistent results that meet or exceed the performance outcomes organizations require from human resource development (HRD). How is it that some HRD practitioners can achieve this state time after time, and others regularly get lost in the process or do not even have a defined HRD process? The contention of this book is that *expert* HRD practitioners think like researchers. You may not need to "officially" be a researcher to obtain consistently high-quality HRD results, but in performing as a true expert you have a large portion of the discipline required to be a researcher (Bereiter & Scardamalia, 1993). Furthermore, professionals who remain out in front of expert practice are likely doing research without knowing it. Thus, the much hyped gap between theory and practice is not something to be scorned or avoided. This perennial gap is the arena of opportunity and excellence: "there is nothing so practical as good research" (Passmore, 1984, p. 24).

Proven principles and theories are as close to truth as we get. They allow us to predict the future better. Without the operating principles and theories—the fruits of research—we have to start over with every problem we face as though it were the first time this problem ever occurred. This causes enormous amounts of inefficiency and ineffectiveness. Many people working in HRD operate this way on the job. For them, every project is approached as a start-up project with an amateurish, *How shall we do this?* question that is void of principles and theories to guide the effort. Without research and its practical use, poor practice in the profession can continue for long periods of time while undermining the credibility of HRD.

Sound Practice: A Practical Benefit of Research

Atheoretical practice is practice that occurs without the guidance of theory. The examples of atheoretical practice and its poor results seem to be everywhere. A recent personal example comes from a very large Fortune 50 corporation. The company surveys about 50,000 employees each year to determine their attitudes, and the theory/research underpinnings are nonexistent. The multiple and conflicting stated purposes of the annual survey undermine each other. It may well be that the survey effort actually hurts the organization rather than helps it. When started some years ago, the survey was loosely but purposefully tied to quality improvement theory and evaluation theory. The external provider of the evaluation services was operating from old and invalid notions about the relationship between satisfaction and performance. Even so, the original overarching quality improvement effort properly utilized the employee survey to *begin* the journey of inquiry, not as an invalid end measure of performance. The quality improvement effort was dismantled but the survey continued. The practice eroded as the theory eroded. The following comments were sent to the vice president of HRD after an on-site visit to review the diminished state of affairs.

> To: HRD Vice President
> From: HRD Consultant
> I appreciated the opportunity to review the status of the company's employee attitude survey (EAS) effort. The review included phone discussions prior to my visit, review of EAS print materials, an on-site visit, and preparation of this abbreviated report.
>
>   You asked for an overview of our exchange to complement these detailed notes of our on-site meeting. Since my comments will take on a problem-solution tone, let me preface them with two very important observations:
>
> ◆ The Company is to be highly commended for its "Vision, Goals, Values" statement. The three goals and their priority of customer, employees, and financial results are right on target from my professional assessment.
> ◆ The company is to be highly commended for investing the energy and resources to systematically collect employee opinions.
>
> The following comments are organized around four issues and the four large opportunities for improvement that have been identified. The problems are as follows:
>
> 1. Unclear expected outcomes of EAS
> 2. Not enough executive level commitment to EAS

3. No documentation or evaluation of EAS outcomes

4. EAS process not under control

Unclear expected outcomes of EAS

EAS should have a very clear expected outcome. At this point, it does not, and this is causing problems. In the EAS documentation there are four inconsistent purposes noted. The origin of the EAS is that it was a sub-component of a quality improvement effort. This was logical. Today that connection is missing, and the EAS has a life of its own without a clearly defined purpose and expected outcome. As is, the EAS can be improved using the specific suggestions provided during my on-site visit. Within those, we talked about (1) reducing the expectations of EAS outcomes to more local and/or personal improvements *or* (2) more rigorously connecting EAS to a defined performance improvement effort.

The core EAS questions are rooted in thirty-to-forty-year-old industrial psychology thinking that has proven to be invalid. The old invalid logic is that satisfied employees become productive employees—therefore get your employees satisfied and then they will be productive. Not true! Today we understand that productive employees who are able to achieve *excellence*, while being treated fairly, will be satisfied employees who in turn will continue to be productive. Thus, the struggle is for *supporting* excellence, not satisfaction.

Most dissatisfied workers are trapped in work places having disjointed work processes and poor organizational leadership that hinders their performance. While satisfaction and productivity are related, satisfaction should be thought of as outcome of excellence and productivity. Thus, helping people achieve excellence has a secondary result—satisfaction. Even though the EAS questions are not the best—given the company's vision, goals, and values—they *could* work if they were truly connected to a substantial performance improvement effort. At this point the existing questions are not connected to a clear goal and, thus, they cause problems.

Not enough executive level commitment to EAS

There is no visible advocate (or champion) of the EAS. This fact positions the EAS as a bureaucratically mandated event. Furthermore, EAS has obviously been structured to not inconvenience those at the top of the corporation and to place the most "burden" on those below. The EAS follow-up action planning process places responsibility on the worker, who lacks corresponding authority to make changes. This perception is aggravated by the nature of the general, high level questions on the EAS that are not directly tied to the work and work setting (e.g., *Compared with other organizations, our insurance benefits are good*). Thus, "high level" survey questions bring out "high level" employees' concerns that are not within the control of the local work group. Yet, employees are charged with attempts to "fix" a perceived problem not in their realm of authority.

No documentation or evaluation of EAS outcomes

There is no systematic evaluation and reporting of EAS improvements (the ultimate outcomes) resulting from acting on the survey data. In that "everything important in business and industry is evaluated," the message in the company is that EAS is an optional activity in terms of importance and managerial follow-through.

EAS process not under control

Employees are rewarded for "lying" on the EAS. If employees say everything is fine, they do not have to deal with it anymore. Review meetings on the survey results can be and are being skipped. Survey results can be delivered to employees without a face-to-face review meeting. Or, the results can be passed out as part of another meeting and quickly dismissed. Additionally, supervisors generally do not have the group process communication skills to run the kind of open dialogue session dealing with attitudes. Thus, many supervisors avoid the meetings.

Those supervisors who do have group process communication skills are likely to be the supporters of the full survey process. Their experience with the EAS is positive in that they are able to make it work for them and their work group.

Mr. VP, your dilemma appears to be what to do for the upcoming survey. The four major points addressed in this report are interconnected and deserve some hard thinking. For example, being precise about outcomes makes evaluation easy as well as provides a basis for clarity in the process and leads logically to an internal champion. The following actions are suggested:

1. Clarify the goal of the EAS and the expected outcomes. The closer the EAS is linked to core business outcomes, the better.
2. Obtain executive level commitment to the EAS in the form of a high level advocate or champion. That person needs to "own" the EAS and the EAS process.
3. Develop a practical evaluation system for EAS outcomes, implement it, and report on the results.
4. Define the EAS process and make it totally consistent with the EAS goal and expected outcomes. Support it with simple, clear documentation and training.

In deciding your next moves, it is critical not to erode the importance of surveying the company's employees. What you have started is important and could add great positive value to the corporation. While I am willing to help in any of these matters, it is best that your company have the internal expertise to deal with these core revisions.

This is an example of practice becoming disengaged from its theory base. To rebuild its value for the organization, the HRD consultant recommends reconnecting the survey to theories of evaluation and performance.

Another example of poor practice as a result of ignoring HRD research has to do with assumptions around trainee satisfaction in relation to learning and job performance. Satisfaction, learning, and performance are separate and worthy *domains* of human resource development evaluation. However, they are not *levels* of evaluation as is widely believed among HRD practitioners and as portrayed by Kirkpatrick's (1994) atheoretical four-level evaluation model (see Holton, 1996; Newstrom, 1995). To be consistent with research, the evaluation domains need to be conceptualized *separately*. Although the domains have some relationship, they are not hierarchical levels of evaluation. Each domain is driven by different assumptions that must be taken into account separately. There can be a relationship among the domains, but it cannot and should not be assumed that the relationship is direct and positive. Contrary to the practitioners' myth, the research shows that participants most satisfied with a program are not necessarily those who learned the most (Alliger & Janak, 1989; Dixon, 1990). High or low satisfaction can be found among low, medium, and high achievers. Furthermore, because participants have gained knowledge and expertise does not mean that they will use it in the workplace (Gielen, 1995).

What is it that drives business and HRD into predictably ignorant (atheoretical) decisions? The pressure to succeed coupled with the pressure of time seem to be the source of many atheoretical decisions. These pressures are preyed upon by marketers of quick fixes to substantive problems. The latest atheoretical marketing flyer to cross my desk is from a large supplier of training films to the huge, lucrative, corporate training sector. Their flyer tells us, "The only constant in our lives today is change" and then goes on to promise what they can deliver with their new video: "A powerful six-minute video shatters people's resistance to change." Who in their theoretically driven mind could do anything but laugh at such a claim? Yet without any knowledge of change theory, or in the absence of commonsense thinking, a six-minute video for $500 may seem like a much needed miracle.

In contrast to the previous example, the disciplined thinking coming from a research perspective helps the practitioner describe and align HRD inputs, processes, and outputs (Swanson, 1994). Just this elementary application of system theory in everyday work would cause an enormous increase in the effectiveness and efficiency of the HRD profession. This is because a large number of the functional disconnects within day-to-day HRD work are caused by well-intentioned but atheoretical practitioners. The six-minute "change" video and the way it is presented may actually cause viewers to dig in their heels and more vigorously resist change rather than "shatter" their resistance, as claimed. From the research and theory on change, I predict that neither will happen.

❖

Definition of Research

Research is often thought of in terms of a job or a task. Actually, research is a *process* having a specific type of outcome. *The outcome of research is new knowledge, obtained through an orderly, investigative process*. The dictionary definition of research is clear and simple: "1. Scholarly or scientific investigation or inquiry; 2. Close and careful study" (Berube, 1982, p. 1051).

Each of you reading this chapter has most likely done research and may even do research on a regular basis in certain arenas of your work and/or personal lives. You may not call it research. Even so, the psychological barriers to officially doing research remain and are typified by (1) the pressures of time limitations and/or (2) the concern over being criticized as to the signifi-

cance, method, or conclusions. It is interesting to note that these
two barriers are the same concerns that haunt the most full-time
and experienced researchers throughout their work. These barriers are part of the human side of the research process.

In dealing with the barriers, researchers talk about the importance of humility and skepticism as attributes of a scholar. Certainly the press of time and the potential of criticism help keep
the researcher humble, and internal skepticism keeps the researcher motivated. Researchers are indeed skeptics *par excellence*. When somebody says, "I know everything will turn out
well," the researcher will retort, "Not necessarily." When somebody says, "I know everything will go badly," the researcher will
similarly retort, "Not necessarily." Untested generalizations do
not satisfy the researcher. They are the *beginnings* of research, not
the conclusions.

The Research Process

Although the general research process starts with a question and
ends with a conclusion, research is not just a problem-solving
method. Problem solving is situational and is judged by results,
with or without a theoretical explanation. If through trial and
error you learn to kick the lawn mower engine to make it start,
the problem of getting the mower engine running is solved without any theoretical understanding. Yet there is a point when
problem solving and the generation of new knowledge touch
and/or overlap. Very thorough and systematic problem solving
that purposefully retains and reports data can at times be thought
of as research. Many people in HRD like to talk about "action
research." Action research would not be considered research by
most researchers. Rather, most researchers would classify action

research as a formalized method of problem solving relevant to a particular organization or setting.

As an applied field, the theory-practice dilemma is of particular importance to HRD. Most HRD scholars recognize *practice-to-theory* to be as true as *theory-to-practice*. HRD scholars should be respectful of the fact that theory often has to catch up to sound practice in that practitioners can be ahead of researchers. Thoughtful practitioners often do things that work, and scholars learn how to explain the successes later. For an applied field such as HRD, the concept of the HRD practitioner being a researcher or research partner is legitimate and crucial to the maturity of the profession.

From my experience in the profession, it is clear that thoughtful and expert practitioners do indeed apply research findings in their day-to-day work decisions. Whether they are *advancing* HRD theory and practice is another matter. It is critical to the profession that thoughtful practitioners recognize that they are in a perfect position to advance the profession through what I call "backyard" research (Swanson, 1996). Backyard research is *systematic investigation and inquiry that is embedded in the ongoing work of the organization*. Backyard researchers are important partners in the scheme of inquiry. The rigorous developmental activities that many practitioners engage in are just a breath away from being research. *Development is the systematic process of perfecting a new kind of product or activity*. By adding a tier of inquiry to the development process, legitimate research emerges! Chapter Three of this book, "HRD Partnerships for Integrating Research and Practice," adds important insights to the working relationship between researchers and practitioners in advancing the profession, whereas Chapter Seven, "Case Study Research Methods," provides methods for studying practice in organizations.

The Theory-Research-Development-Practice Cycle

Theory, research, development, and practice together compose a vital cycle that allows ideas to be progressively refined as they evolve from concepts to practices and from practices to concepts. The *Theory-Research-Development-Practice cycle* illustrates the systematic application of inquiry methods working to advance the knowledge used by both HRD researchers and practitioners (see Swanson, 1988).

Although we find no historical evidence in the philosophy of science that an *a priori* linkage among theory, research, development, and practice was ever established, such a relationship has emerged within and across professional disciplines. For HRD, the call to inform practice with theory, research, and development has come relatively recently (Passmore, 1984; Swanson, 1988; Gradous, 1989). In other fields of study, there has been a longer tradition of pursuing theory, research, development, and practice in ways that are mutually beneficial to each element.

However, there are those that caution us in constructing the relationships among theory, research, development, and practice. In offering the notion of a scientific *paradigm*, Kuhn (1970) compelled philosophers and researchers to rethink the assumptions underlying the scientific method and paved the way for alternative, postpositivistic approaches to research in the behavioral sciences. Ethnography and naturalistic inquiry allow theory to *emerge from data derived from practice and experience;* theory does not necessarily precede research as theory can be generated through it. The model of theory, research, development, and practice for HRD embraces these cautions (see Figure 1.1).

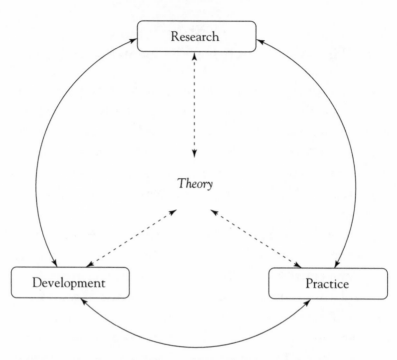

Figure 1.1. Theory-Research-Development-Practice Cycle

The cyclical model brings HRD theory, research, development, and practice together in the same forum. The union of these domains is itself an important purpose of the model. Two other purposes also exist. First, each of the four domains makes a necessary contribution to effective HRD. There is no presumption about the relative value to the profession of contributions from practice versus theory. The model demonstrates the need for all domains to inform each other in order to enrich the profession as a whole. Second, exchange among the domains is multidirectional. Any of the domains can serve as an appropriate starting point for proceeding through the cycle. Improvements in the profession can occur whether one begins with theory, research, development, or practice.

HRD Research: Don't Go to Work Without It!

The process of working through the Theory-Research-Development-Practice cycle demonstrates how any of the four domains can be used as a starting point for knowledge generation in HRD. As a starting point of the cycle, *research* is undertaken to expand our professional knowledge base and frequently yields recommendations for the development of new systems or the improvement of practice. This link from *research* to *practice* is illustrated by influential research that has yielded innovative models of job design, work motivation, performance analysis, organizational change, and other products of research that have led directly to improvements in the profession.

Research can also proceed along the cycle to produce *theory*. Theory building is an important function of research that will be addressed in a later chapter. Although HRD has benefited from a rich foundation of theories, many of which originated in related fields of study, additional theories of HRD are needed for greater understanding of a wide range of human and organizational phenomena. Thus, research serves a dual role in advancing HRD knowledge: it provides knowledge that can be directly applied to the improvement of practice, and it is used to develop core theories of HRD.

HRD *development* efforts offer a unique opportunity to enter the cycle. Excessive demands on organizations and HRD practice are the primary drivers of new models and methods of doing HRD work. HRD is a system within a larger system and they each influence one another to the point that practical new ways of organizing for and/or developing HRD interventions become natural starting points of activity and inquiry.

Examples of *development* efforts that have stimulated advances in the profession (theory, research, and practice) have come from large-scale change efforts, military training challenges, HRD issues facing multinational corporations, and the introduction of new information technologies. In this realm of research, a rigorous HRD development process is needed to ensure quality, and this is more important than the generalizability of the effectiveness of the end product. For example, Sayre's (1990) research on the development and evaluation of a computer-based system for managing the design and pilot testing of interactive videodiscs necessarily invested much more effort in the realm of *development* than in what we would classify as formal *research*.

When starting with HRD *practice*, there is no shortage of problems and challenges facing HRD. These challenges provide an inexhaustible source of researchable problems. Proceeding from practice-to-research or practice-to-development along the cycle traces a familiar path among problems that continuously arise in organizations and the research and development efforts they stimulate. For example, research is often stimulated by the need for organizations to improve HRD practices and their effectiveness. New teaching methods, new group process techniques, and alternative providers of services are just some of the reoccurring practice options. Other problems occur when new technical systems are acquired before personnel have the expertise to use them. Research continues to identify effective ways of developing the expertise to take advantage of emerging technologies. Scores of other HRD research projects are undertaken to address pressing problems of practice.

Each of the domains of the Theory-Research-Development-Practice cycle serves to advance the HRD profession. Each can be a catalyst to inquiry and a source of validation.

The cycle frequently starts with *theory* when it is used to guide and inform the processes of research, development, or practice. The variables and relationships to be considered are identified by reviewing the literature, which includes relevant theory. For example, if we wish to examine the influence of recent changes in work design on work motivation, we might start with existing theories of work motivation and identify variables from these theories that are relevant to our question. In the realm of work analysis, Torraco (1994) challenged this large area of professional activity as being highly researched but essentially atheoretical.

In summary, the process of knowledge generation can begin at any point along the Theory-Research-Development-Practice cycle and can flow in several directions. The researcher or practitioner can start at any point and proceed in any direction. Thus, each of the cycle's domains both *informs* and *is informed by* each of the other domains.

This continuum provides a context for theory that helps to explain why theory has so many important roles. Whether one is an HRD researcher or practitioner, theory serves several roles that can greatly enhance the effectiveness of our work.

Importance of Reporting Research

If a tree falls in the forest and nobody is there, does it make any sound? Remember that philosophy puzzler? Oddly, the dissemination of research findings poses a similar problem. If research is conducted, and it is not disseminated, is there new knowledge? Reporting the results is the last step in a research project. There are two threats to completing this last step in the research process. One threat has to do with the human frailties of the researcher. The researcher has learned what he or she wanted to learn and is ready to move on, has found no significant differences (actually this is very valuable knowledge), or is still worried about facing external criticism. These personal barriers often result in valuable but unreported data.

The second threat has to do with dissemination outlets. Dissemination outlets create what appear to be ominous barriers with unfamiliar manuscript and publication requirements, particularly for the neophyte researcher. Here are three suggestions. First, get a partner, someone who has been through the hoops. Second, produce a one- or two-page executive summary; some will be interested in a full report, more will be interested in a journal article report, and most will be interested in the executive summary. Third, submit your final report to the ERIC Clearinghouse, a massive database of studies that come in a variety of formats and are made available to the public on microfilm. Use the information below to contact them:

ERIC Clearinghouse
Reproduction Service
3900 Wheeler Ave.
Arlington, VA 22304
Phone: (800) 227–3742

Getting Help with Your Research

Although research can be a lonely process, there is no reason to be alone in the effort. There are many organizations capable of assisting you in your research. Almost every university has an office of research and individual faculty members interested and capable of partnering with you. There are a limited number of organizations dedicated to human resource development research. Here are two:

Academy of Human Resource Development
P.O. Box 25113
Baton Rouge, LA 70894
Phone: (504) 334–1874; Fax: (504) 334–1875;
e-mail: office @ahrd.org

Research Committee
American Society for Training and Development
1640 King St., P.O. Box 1443
Alexandria, VA 22313
Phone: (703) 683–8100; Fax: (703) 683–8103

You, the Researcher

How do you approach the notion of being a researcher? Do you view it as a transition, analogous to the moth that becomes a butterfly? Or do you view it as a compartmentalized segment of human activity? The notion of being a backyard researcher assumes that you can engage in research in a compartmentalized manner and within a small or specific realm. Remember, many part-timers in almost any realm can be terrific at what they do even though they do not engage in the activity day in and day out. The neophyte and/or part-time researcher should keep the following points in mind as a project is being planned: don't make it too risky, keep it small, get help, and have fun.

The following chapters in this book are intended to provide the overview and basic tools required to begin the journey of thinking and performing as a researcher. As you begin the journey, remember: research is neither inherently easy nor difficult; research requires inquisitiveness and follow-through; and research and its benefits are very practical.

References

Bereiter, C., & Scardamalia, M. (1993). *Surpassing ourselves: An inquiry into the nature and implications of expertise.* Chicago: Open Court.

Dixon, N. M. (1990). Relationship between trainees' responses on participant reaction forms and their posttest achievement score. *Human Resource Development Quarterly, 1*(2), 129–137.

Gielen, E. (1995). *Transfer of training in a corporate setting*. Enschede, The Netherlands: University of Twente.

Gradous, D. B. (Ed.). (1989). *Systems theory applied to human resource development*. Alexandria, VA: American Society for Training and Development Press.

Holton, E. F. III. (1996). The flawed four-level evaluation model. *Human Resource Development Quarterly, 7*(1), 23–25.

Kirkpatrick, D. L. (1994). *Evaluating training programs: The four levels*. San Francisco: Berrett-Koehler.

Kuhn, T. S. (1970). *The structure of scientific revolutions* (2nd ed.). Chicago: University of Chicago Press.

McClernon, T., & Swanson, R. A. (1995). Effects of computer-based support on team building with management and work groups. *Human Resource Development Quarterly, 6*(1), 39–58.

Newstrom, J. W. (1995). Review of Evaluating training programs: The four levels. *Human Resource Development Quarterly, 6*(3), 317–320.

Nicholas, S., & Langseth, R. W. (1982). The comparative impact of organization development interventions on hard criteria measures. *Academy of Management Review, 7*(2), 531–542.

Passmore, D. L. (1984). Nothing more practical than good research. *Performance and Instruction Journal, 22*(10), 24.

Sayre, S. (1990). *The development and evaluation of a computer-based system for managing the design and pilot testing of interactive videodisks program*. St. Paul: University of Minnesota, Human Resource Development Research Center.

Swanson, R. A. (1988). Research and development (and other life and death matters). *Performance Improvement Quarterly, 1*(1), 69–82.

Swanson, R. A. (1994). *Analysis for improving performance: Tools for diagnosing organizations and documenting workplace expertise*. San Francisco: Berrett-Koehler.

Torraco, R. J. (1994). *A theory of work analysis*. St. Paul: University of Minnesota, Human Resource Development Research Center.

C H A P T E R

How Research Contributes to the HRD Value Chain

Michael P. Leimbach
Wilson Learning Corporation

Timothy T. Baldwin
Indiana University

Probably at least half of every training dollar we spend is wasted—we just don't know which half.

—A corporate training manager

What human resource development (HRD) questions can be addressed by research strategies? The simple but not very useful answer is, all and none! If the purpose of an HRD intervention is to improve organizational or individual performance, research—by itself—will not accomplish the goal. However, research will enhance any HRD intervention, improving its efficiency, effectiveness, and impact on the organization, team, or individual.

One way to think of the purpose of research in HRD practice is to imagine a catalyst in a chemical reaction. In its simplest form, chemistry is the combining of two or more chemicals to make a new chemical. However, in many chemical reactions, the original chemicals, like oil and water, do not naturally combine. But a third ingredient, the catalyst, can provide the necessary environment that allows for the original chemicals to combine and form the new chemical. HRD research, like the catalyst, does not itself improve organizational performance, but in most cases it is a necessary catalyst to ensure that the other elements of the HRD intervention interact in a meaningful way.

Whether we call it performance analysis, front-end analysis, needs analysis, impact analysis, or some other term, there is an unfortunate dearth of research-based prescriptions for HRD professionals who would like to incorporate research strategies into their efforts to improve organizational performance. Of course, authors have long lamented that much of current HRD practice is far more art than science, but the problem is particularly acute with respect to HRD research strategies. Indeed, Rossett (1992) postulated that if 100 human performance professionals were given the same organizational information and situation, they would be likely to come up with 100 different solution proposals yielding 100 different results! Although that may be something of an exaggeration, there is clearly a need for attention devoted to the identification and illustration of various organizational HRD research approaches.

The objective of this chapter, therefore, is to take advantage of our academic/practitioner partnership to link recent conceptual work on the application of research with the reality of progressive HRD practices. We will focus on the uses of research in HRD practice. What we will not be specifically addressing are uses of research in theory building and hypothesis testing. This is not to discount the importance of theory building and hypothesis testing to the science of HRD, which are in fact critical to the advancement of the field. However, for the practitioner, the primary role of research lies in advancing the organizational practices and secondarily in advancing the field scientifically. This tension between research in the service of practice and research in the service of science will be more fully explored in Chapter Three.

Human Resource Development Value Chain

The strategy of the company, the direction of the company, and the skills and behaviors that people need . . . should all be combined and integrated. The toughest problem that training professionals have within a company is how to interpret and integrate new ideas into the training and how to do it quickly.

—David Kearns, CEO, Xerox [Galagan, 1990]

The significance of research applications to HRD is, in part, the degree to which the research process meets certain characteristics alluded to in David Kearn's quote. In fact, HRD research is a primary way in which HRD is linked to the broader organizational goals. Research has the potential of translating HRD activities into the language of business in a way no other HRD function can. This creates an increasing demand for HRD researchers to think and act like business managers. They need to understand, on a deep level, how their organization creates value. They need to understand vital business data and how to extract information from financial reports. They need to remain aware of new products, structures, equipment, and people. Most important, all HRD professionals should seek to understand their organization's value chain and how different parts of the organization add value to the products and services produced.

The way an organization creates value for customers has been described as a value chain that begins with the conceptualization of an idea and proceeds through the customers' use of that idea in its commercialized form (Porter, 1985). Each step in this chain (design, development, manufacturing, marketing, sales, delivery, etc.) adds value to the preceding step. The value created by the organization results not from the individual elements but from the integration of the elements, linked by their common support of the organization's strategic intent.

HRD, along with finance, administration, purchasing, and other functions, is seen as a support system to the primary value chain that defines a business. However, like the primary value chain, HRD also has a value chain that defines the way it contributes value to the individual and the organization. The HRD value chain is defined by its ability to create human capability for achieving the vision of success for the organization and its business units. Thus, integration with organizational strategy is central to human resource development's ability to deliver value. The components of HRD must be aligned and focused on organizational success (Figure 2.1). Elements of HRD are less about serving particular functions (selection, training) and more about delivering capabilities for creating value.

As a core competency, HRD research contributes to all segments of the HRD value chain. We have chosen to describe the

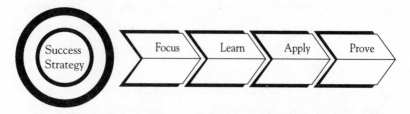

Figure 2.1. Human Resource Development Value Chain

purposes of research within HRD by using this value chain analogy. In addition to providing a context for positioning HRD research as a link to strategy, the value chain analogy also helps illustrate that part of the value of research is its ability to link the elements of the HRD value chain. By implementing research designs that address all elements of the value chain, you integrate research into all aspects of how HRD contributes value and link that research to organizational strategic intent.

Within this context, we see four principal areas where HRD research contributes to the value created by HRD. Although research undoubtedly will contribute to other elements of HRD, the most critical are as follows:

Focus: Proving focus and direction to HRD efforts and linking them to the strategic focus of the organization. This encompasses what has been traditionally referred to as needs analysis, needs assessment, front-end analysis, and other processes that help define and prioritize developmental needs.

Learn: Enhancing learning through the application of research methods in the learning process. This involves feedback and 360–degree assessment, analytical exercises, and action research methodologies.

Apply: Enhancing the transfer of learning to the workplace through research. This involves follow-up research applications and diagnosis of transfer climate issues.

Prove: Determining the impact of HRD initiatives on organizational and individual performance. This incorporates evaluation studies, return on investment, and other methods for proving that HRD contributes to organizational and financial success.

This chapter addresses the characteristics of these four purposes, or contributions, of research to the HRD value chain. In addition, we propose that it is the linking of these purposes that provides the greatest contribution of research. The chapter ends with an example of how one research approach was used to fulfill all four elements of the value chain and the impact of this on the organization.

Characteristics of Effective Research

In applying research strategies to these four purposes (focus, learn, apply, prove), we have reached some conclusions concerning the general characteristics that determine the effectiveness of research practices. Regardless of the specific purpose, we have found that the following are critical considerations in assuring that HRD research contributes to, rather than hinders, organizational performance.

Research should be customer driven. Although a customer-driven perspective is hardly novel in organizations today, our experience is that the concept of customer-driven HRD has only recently come to the fore. In our experience, most HRD research efforts have taken a far more narrow and internal focus than a customer-driven model would suggest. From a customer-driven perspective, the most fundamental, but often neglected, HRD question is, who is the client or customer for the research? As Robinson and Robinson (1989) note, for much of existing HRD practices an honest answer to the question would suggest that no one can truly be specified as the client. That is, there would be no one individual or group outside of the HRD function who values, asks for, or has something significant to gain or lose from the outcomes of the research intervention. The client could be senior officers of the firm, a line manager, or even truly external customers. Regardless of who the customer is, we would argue that it is crucial that a customer be identified for every HRD research initiative. Even more important, HRD providers should strive to forge a partnership in order to understand the vision of success for those clients—not just for HRD but for the clients' business in general.

Research should be linked to value creation. From the perspective of the firm, there really are no "development" problems per se, only business problems—for which HRD might be one strategy or system component for creating value for customers or owners. HRD will be most successful when it is understood that its primary concern is with the success of the business and that learning is a means to an end. In this vein, a common and often justified criticism leveled at human resource professionals in general, and HRD researchers in particular, has been that they have not "understood the business." Regardless of the historical truth of that indictment, it seems clear that in today's competitive reality an understanding of the business has become essential. In this regard, every research effort should begin with an understanding of the strategic intent associated with the problem or issue under investigation. In other words, the researcher should be able to answer the question, How is this effort contributing to the creation of value?   *Big Pic*

Research time frames should be short. Changing market demands drive changing organizational structures, which in turn drive the need for changing skills and abilities. There is a perception (and to some degree a reality) that systematic HRD research has traditionally taken so long that once the research is done, the skills and practices are no longer important because jobs and markets have changed. This perception no doubt accounts for why informal discussions, observations, and interviews are the most commonly used research tools (Ralphs & Stephan, 1986). The most effective HRD research strategies consider the time-value they provide, not just the information-value.

Research should maintain rigor. One of the paradoxes of the HRD research role is the pull between rigor and speed. Informal methodologies are certainly fast ways to identify some of the most critical general issues. However, informal methods tend to identify only the most obvious solutions. As we know, "for every problem there is an answer that is obvious, easy, and wrong" (with our apologies to Mark Twain). Of course, many organizations do recognize the advantages of rigorous analysis. We suspect that the disinterest in systematic research many be more an issue of time than of money or desire. Therefore, improvement in the rigor of research will only occur when we are able to reduce the time between when a decision maker in an organization asks a question and when the researcher can provide an actionable answer. In short, contributing to organizational success requires addressing more than the easily identified issues. The only way to ensure that the less obvious but important human research development issues are addressed is to incorporate more rigorous research processes into the practice of human resource development. But how do we do so without lengthening the time? One critical element is to recognize that the "time" being referred to is the time from when the organization's management asks the question to when the researcher can provide an answer. It is not necessarily the time of a research project from start to finish.

The next four sections of this chapter focus in detail on the four principle areas in the HRD value chain: Focus, Learn, Apply, and Prove.

Focus Research

It is hardly provocative to suggest that a process of systematically identifying, understanding, and prioritizing development needs is critical to effective HRD. Just as no competent surgeon would operate without a thorough diagnosis of the patient, few HRD professionals today would consider an HRD intervention without some form of organizational needs analysis. These questions are asked more frequently in organizations than ever before, for example, Which development needs are most critical to organizational success? How do we allocate our scarce HRD dollars? What HRD interventions might serve to best drive change in our organization? Although to "do things right" in terms of the design and delivery of HRD remains crucial, it is also critical to "do the right things" in the first place. In short, determining the *Focus* of HRD needs, and the potential contribution of HRD initiatives to organizational effectiveness, are of paramount concern in today's business reality.

Few question the value of Focus research, but there is an unfortunate dearth of research on the best approach to fulfill this purpose. What are the characteristics of an effective needs analysis strategy? Although far from a definitive answer, our experience suggests that the following considerations are of prime importance.

Focus on Organizational Strategy

In today's business reality, needs analysis research efforts that focus exclusively on importance of skills to a job or actions to a function are fundamentally flawed. Teams are rapidly displacing individual workers as a basis unit of performance, the flow of work is increasingly cross-functional, and job responsibilities are changing frequently to meet new demands. Therefore, needs analysis processes should focus less on identifying the skills of a job and more on identifying the competencies required to achieve organizational strategic objectives. One approach to this is represented in Figure 2.2.

Figure 2.2. Aligning Strategies and Competencies

A key element to linking a needs analysis or Focus research efforts to strategic intent is understanding the market conditions in which your client operates—that is, understanding your customer's customer. Whether these are external customers or internal customers, many business problems or needs are a result of changing business conditions, especially changing markets. We have found that gathering information on the customer's customer is a key element to a successful research effort. This means that every needs analysis should gather information directly from the customer's customer.

To focus a training and development effort requires knowing what to focus on. By this we mean that every needs analysis process needs to identify and clarify the business target of the initiative. The question, What business problem or need is addressed by this intervention? must be posed and the learning objectives tied back to this target.

Also critical to a successful intervention is an analysis of and linkage with the distinctive or "core competencies" of a firm.

Core competencies are defined as the combination of individual technologies and operational skills that underlie a company's product and service lines. For example, Cannon's core competency in optics, imaging, and microprocessor controls has enabled it to enter markets as seemingly diverse as copiers, image scanners, cameras, and laser printers. And J. P. Morgan's scope of international thinking and work, based on established leadership in globally linked markets, has distinguished its approach to global financial intermediation for more than a century. If a firm's competitive advantage is derived from distinctive capabilities of the workforce, then it seems clear that the most important HRD interventions will be those that focus on and support further developments of these core competencies.

Provide Just-in-Time Information

As indicated at the beginning of this chapter, shortening cycle time is important to the effectiveness of HRD research. This is especially important for Focus research. Often active interventions await the results of the needs analysis, and to executive and line managers this often feels like treading water. Any activity that can increase the immediacy of the results will have value. There are several methods for accomplishing this objective.

If you collect data before the question is asked, then the answer will come much more quickly. This may sound trite, but successful research can be conducted by anticipating questions and beginning the data collection process before the issue is actually verbalized. By monitoring business literature, industry trends, and any changes in the organization's strategy and resources, the HRD professional can formulate research questions and select those with the highest probability of occurrence. By anticipating questions and having responses already under investigation, cycle time can be dramatically reduced.

Conducting research in phases can also reduce perceived cycle time. Successful needs analysis research has been conducted by designing the first phase to identify the most obvious issues and begin addressing them immediately. Then the more complete analysis can be performed to address the less obvious but important issues. Because most HRD interventions occur over time, research and program delivery are simultaneous.

A third way to reduce cycle time is to make use of existing tools. For example, research indicates that there is a great deal of consistency among management competency models across organizations and industries (Zingheim, Ledford, & Schuster, 1996). The research professional can save significant time by utilizing existing competency models, rather than re-creating them through lengthy competency analysis.

Actively involving the target audience can also shorten the perceived data analysis time. On several occasions, one of the authors has used preliminary data from the customer's customer input to construct a workshop during which an electronic group decision support tool (GDSS; see Poole, 1991, for more detailed description) was used to collect data on the skills and competencies needed to address the customer's needs. The workshop participants view the workshop as a learning intervention (some have even expressed that it was "the best training program that they have been to"), and the data provided an effective basis for a competency needs analysis.

❖

Learn Research

It is ironic that the most used purpose of research is also the one that is least well researched. We are referring to the use of research methods to directly assist the learning process. The vast majority of this comes in the form of instrumentation (questionnaires, surveys) that provides people with feedback or insight into the competencies being learned. This ranges from simple in-class surveys to complex 360–degree feedback instruments.

It is an underestimation to say that thousands of program participants receive some type of research-based feedback each week. Anecdotal evidence indicates that participants often view feedback as the most useful and memorable element of a program. Yet despite the popularity of such feedback, there is almost no research available on what makes a good instrument for learning purposes or what value such instruments deliver.

Feedback measurement can assist learning in many ways. Feedback instrument results can motivate learning. Most people take pride in performing their jobs well and take pleasure in learning new skills that will improve their performance. Such people often find it deeply satisfying to be able to measure their own progress through instrument-guided training. Also, skepticism about the value of a particular development effort can dissolve in the face of concrete, measurable improvement in skills. Instruments allow employees to take more control over their own training, because they provide them with a method of assessing the outcome of their own learning efforts.

Feedback instruments are also a way to tailor learning to the individual. One problem in delivering training programs is that even when a need has been identified, there will be variability in skill within individuals in a program session. The result is that people feel that the program is generic and not necessarily suited to them. Instrument-guided learning provides each participant with unique information on his or her own strengths and weaknesses. This helps the participants to see the value of the content for them personally and greatly enhances the effectiveness of the learning.

Another approach to using research methods to address the Learn element of the HRD value chain is by incorporating action research approaches into the learning methodologies. Proponents of action research emphasize that the act of doing research is an effective learning tool. For example, organizations have effectively changed leadership culture within their organizations by having workshop participants actively research leadership practices; interview well-known effective leaders; and design, implement, and analyze questionnaires from employees who rate different managers and leader competencies.

Apply Research

Traditional research strategies have focused largely on needs analysis (Focus) and evaluation (Prove). However, recent research suggests that the failure of learned skills to transfer to the workplace is because of the failure of systems to support the transfer of learning (Baldwin & Ford, 1988). We contend that it would be useful to reconceptualize research approaches to include examination of systemwide components that determine whether a training program can yield meaningful change back on the job.

Unfortunately, there are no frameworks for researching or measuring the characteristics of organizations, individuals, or work environment that contribute most to the application of learning to the workplace. One interesting stream of research is that dealing with transfer environments (Baldwin & Magjuka, 1991; Rouillier & Goldstein, 1993). For example, Rouillier and Goldstein (1993) have hypothesized a set of supervisory and organizational characteristics, which they have termed *transfer climate.* Transfer climate consists of two general categories: (1) situational cues and (2) consequences. Situational cues consist of things such as manager goals, peer support, equipment availability, and opportunity for practice. Consequences consist of punishment and positive and negative feedback. In their study of transfer climate, Rouillier and Goldstein (1993) studied the transfer climate of 102 fast food franchise locations. Assistant manager trainees, after completing a nine-week training program, were randomly assigned to one of the 102 organizational units. Results indicated that trainees assigned to units with a more positive transfer climate demonstrated more trained behavior on the job (Rouillier & Goldstein, 1993).

Using some of Rouillier and Goldstein's items, another team of researchers (Tracey, Tannenbaum, & Kavanaugh, 1995) identified a set of nine factors affecting the transfer of learning to the workplace that were similar but not identical to Rouillier and Goldstein's (1993). In another approach to application research, Baldwin and Magjuka (1991) found that certain types of managerial behavior (e.g., mandatory attendance, pretraining information, posttraining accountability) also lead to higher intentions to transfer training to the job.

The general lesson for HRD researchers is that it is time to explicitly address the social environmental and organizational context of learning activities. This does not mean abandoning the core of traditional research practices, but it does mean more careful attention to variables that have been ignored or controlled. Rather than generating additional ways to exclude these questions from study, HRD researchers need to explore how these context factors interact with training design elements to help or hinder program success. Practitioners, in collaboration with researchers, can identify the contextual constraints and barriers they face in applying learning in the workplace, and their insights can shape research designs that produce knowledge useful to theory and practice.

Unfortunately, study of the contextual influences on transfer climate is not widely conducted. This appears to be a critical missing step in the contribution of research to the HRD value chain. Most organizations use some type of postcourse participant reaction form ("smile sheet") at the completion of a program. These reaction forms provide little value to evaluation impact or outcomes. If HRD research practitioners began examining not the participants' reactions to the training but their expectations as to the degree to which application/transfer will be supported, this critical link in the value chain can be filled without significant loss in important information.

Prove Research

Probably one of the most discussed topics in HRD research over the past few years has been how to prove the impact of HRD on individual and organizational outcomes. There are several competing models for how to position or discuss impact evaluation. Probably the most widely known model is the one introduced by Donald Kirkpatrick (1996). This model, usually referred to as the Kirkpatrick or four-level model, identifies a taxonomy of four outcome types (reactions, knowledge, behavior, results). However, although the four-level model is widely acknowledged, it is does not truly provide a model that allows us to test learning assumptions and predict learning outcomes (Holton, 1996).

Over the past several years, researchers have set aside the four-level model and focused on Return-on-Investment, utility analysis, and forecasting the economic benefits of learning system (e.g., Swanson & Sawzin, 1976; Schmidt, Hunter, & Pearl, 1982; Swanson & Gradous, 1988; Sheppeck & Cohen, 1985; Leimbach & Morical, 1990). More recently, these and other approaches to determining the economic value of learning have been criticized as being too speculative and indirect measures of impact.

In an effort to integrate some of the diverse literature encompassed under proving the impact of training and development, we offer this framework for organizing the research options.

The first element that is unique about this framework, compared to other evaluation models, is that it considers the complexity of the learning design. Not all learning interventions are created equal. Simple learning solutions consist of isolated training programs or public seminars with little support for the transfer of the learning. Complex solutions might involve groupwide kick-off meetings, following by individualized development plans, 360–degree feedback, and ongoing application support. Most interventions lie somewhere in between these with varying levels of organizational and transfer support.

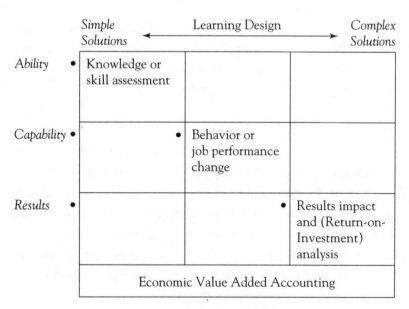

	Simple Solutions	Learning Design	Complex Solutions
Ability •	Knowledge or skill assessment		
Capability •		• Behavior or job performance change	
Results •			• Results impact and (Return-on-Investment) analysis
	Economic Value Added Accounting		

Figure 2.3. Proving Impact Model

There is an underlying assumption that the more extensive the instructional design, the deeper the level of impact; that is, different learning designs are likely to produce different levels of impact. This model defines three levels of impact.

1. *Ability impact.* Increase in knowledge or ability but not direct application. Examples of ability measures include in-class exercises, knowledge-gain tests, and skill-application tests.
2. *Capability impact.* Increase in job performance. Examples of capability measures include behavior change instruments, job performance measures, supervisor interviews, and performance appraisals.
3. *Business results.* Increase in business performance or critical success factor measures. Examples of business results measures include revenue increases, profit margin gains, improved quality, and increased customer satisfaction.

For example, an organization is not likely to see business results improve if the learning design consists of only a simple program solution. Therefore, it is important to match the level of impact measured to the solution design.

Ability Research

Because there is little support for the transfer of learning to the workplace in simple solutions, the best approach to proving the impact is to focus on ability measures. Knowledge tests and skill assessments are the most often used approaches to measuring the impact of an individual learning program. In its simplest form, a knowledge or skill test is given before the program and then immediately after the program. Improved test scores indicate the amount of learning created by the program.

Capability Research

Since moderately complex programs usually provide at least some support for the transfer of learning to the job, a more appropriate approach to proving impact is a capability measure. Capability measures consist of behavioral feedback instrumentation, job products, simulations of work activities, or direct observations. In its basic form, capability research involves a prelearning measure of capability and then an appropriate delay after the initiation of learning to allow the new skills to emerge, followed by a postlearning measure. Improved performance scores indicate the amount of learning created by the program.

Results and ROI Analysis

For learning systems that are fully integrated into the performance improvement process for the organization, a results level, or Return-on-Investment (ROI) analysis is the best approach to proving impact. There are numerous methods for measuring and estimating ROI of training and development and detailed descriptions as cited earlier. However, there are certain characteristics that make ROI studies more or less difficult.

ROI analysis is more easily conducted for jobs that are more directly involved in value creation or value delivery. For example, salespeople (quotas, total sales, market share), customer service representatives (customer satisfaction and retention), and production line groups (defect rates, production rates, quality control measures) can be more easily tied to economic measures of performance than accounting or middle management jobs.

Result measures that are more directly tied to the learning objectives are better than those that are less direct. For example, customer relationship training for sales or service people is best evaluated with measures of customer satisfaction and retention data than sales and market share data because the impact of the training on sales is indirect, via the ability to create greater satisfaction.

Economic Value Added

A final element of research on measuring the impact of training and development is the concept of Economic Value Added (EVA). EVA has been captivating managers of large organizations recently because of its ability to handle the difficult business valuations required to focus all of the firm's activities on shareholder value (Copeland, Koller, & Murrin, 1990).

To briefly illustrate, according to today's accounting treatment, all training expenses are immediately charged to the income statement, suggesting that all training has a life of no more than one year, an assumption we find completely invalid. Surely, many training activities have payoffs that last beyond one year. However, according to the precepts of EVA, training expenditures should be capitalized on the balance sheet as an equity equivalent and then amortized into earnings over the anticipated payoff period. In the EVA system, training is properly viewed as an investment, which many training professionals have long advocated, and the cost of training is included as an amortized expense in the income statement, much like depreciation.

Under the EVA way of thinking, there is no incentive to radically cut or eliminate training budgets as a reaction to a temporary business downturn. Likewise, a company that grows its training budget over time will show a growing asset on its balance sheet, exactly like a company growing its physical asset base of plant and equipment. Clearly, those HRD interventions deemed most important and most likely to receive senior management funding and support will be those with a demonstrated link to value-adding activity in the firm. Over time, the training asset is amortized and loses its value unless replenished. An EVA system ensures against the typical short-term thinking that sometimes is used in cutting the training budget.

The analog to physical equipment investment that is not replenished is clear. The business must return an appropriate earning on its investment, whether that investment be research and development (R&D), advertising, HRD, etc. If the goal of HRD is to ultimately improve business unit performance, then training budgets and all EVA performance measures should be done on that basis. Regardless of whether the firm formally adopts an EVS perspective, advocacy of HRD as a contributor to shareholder value would be an exceptionally valuable addition to the HRD analyst's tool kit.

Integrating Research Through the Value Chain: A Case Study

In this chapter, we have suggested that the most effective method of incorporating research into an HRD strategy is to integrate research into every element of the value chain. Although it is possible to apply research to isolated segments of the value chain, it is our belief that the impact of research on HRD is significantly enhanced when the researcher plans a single strategy for addressing all of the segments as an integrated research effort. By linking research approaches to the complete value chain, the researcher becomes a strategic partner in performance improvement. With this in mind, we would like to describe one example that shows how a single research effort can be integrated in the Focus, Learning, Apply, and Prove elements of the HRD value chain.

This case involved a large manufacturer of industrial products that had recently reorganized and realigned a series of product lines. In the past, customers preferred to purchase their products as independent components. Now, customers were seeking integrated solutions that combined products across product lines. With this systems approach came new competitors, many providing products at lower costs. The company found itself needing to meet increasingly higher expectations for quality, increased expertise on the part of the buyer, and downward cost pressure. With the new competition, it was becoming evident that the traditional sources of competitive advantage that the organization had relied upon were disappearing. The organization's strategy was to find ways to make the sales force a primary source of competitive advantage.

As a result, a new sales division was created out of what were formerly three separate divisions. Salespeople were faced with learning a broader line of products with complex system configurations in an increasingly competitive environment. It was clear to the vice president of sales that the need-based sales process and skills they had been using were not meeting these requirements. In addition, sales management soon recognized that the salespeople from the three divisions all had different types and levels of sales training.

In this situation, the design team did not feel that the salespeople and managers were the best source of information on what skills were needed. For most of them, this was a new market and a new level of competition. Therefore, the research effort began with a review of literature on competition. Drawing not only from sales literature but also from marketing and even sports and military strategy, the design team developed a model describing the outcomes, behaviors, and knowledge they thought the salespeople needed. It was a developmental model in that it described the behaviors, knowledge, and outcomes at three levels of development representing different levels of behavioral complexity.

The research focused not so much on the job of salesperson as on the requirements for creating a new source of advantage in a highly competitive environment. By focusing on the competencies rather than the job, we were able to explore a range of behaviors, knowledge, and skill that would not have been visible in a traditional job or needs analysis. Thus, this perspective required researchers to start from a strategic objective (creating a new source of competitive advantage) using the research strategy to link the HRD intervention to strategic intent.

A series of questionnaires was developed using this model. The measurement process followed a multiple-source (360–degree) design. The questionnaires were completed by salespeople, sales managers, customers, and sales executives. Upon completion of data collection, the results were analyzed to determine the priority organizational development needs. Results indicated that the organization's greatest challenge was the lack of consultative selling skills required in their highly complex and competitive sales environment. The analysis further specified the behavioral outcomes that the training had to address. From this analysis, the researchers worked with the curriculum developers to utilize the research to "Focus" design and development efforts.

Once the curriculum design team selected a set of initiatives to address priority issues and identified existing training and development materials that could address less critical organizational needs, the data were again used to support the "Learn" segment of the value chain. A set of workshop sessions was scheduled with salespeople and managers. The data were reprocessed so that individual feedback reports could be provided to salespeople for individual learning guidance. In these sessions, salespeople were introduced to the concept of a salesperson as a source of competitive advantage and provided with their personal 360–degree feedback. In addition, we were able to provide salespeople with a personalized listing of learning materials and programs based upon their own needs. During the workshop, salespeople developed a learning plan and prepared for a meeting with their managers to discuss the plan.

In addition, a series of manager sessions was conducted. In these sessions, managers were provided with sales unit feedback and specific coaching suggestions, again based upon their own sales units' priority needs identified in the 360–degree measurement. Managers were also provided with instruction in how to conduct coaching sessions. In addition, a sales opportunity analysis work sheet, based upon the research model, was introduced. This sales opportunity analysis work sheet provided a tool for managers to reinforce the learning of the new skills by guiding a discussion between the manager and the salesperson on every new sales opportunity then encountered. Thus, this research design also played a significant role in supporting the "Apply" segment of the value chain.

Finally, eighteen months later, the original 360–degree measurement was repeated along with measures of revenue, revenue increases since training began, and quota achievement goals. The results of the follow-up measurement indicated that there were significant improvements in the sales competencies and that the sales competencies were significantly related to sales performance. In fact, the results indicated that 31 percent of the variance in sales performance could be accounted for by improvements in the sales competencies.

Although numerous other research methods and designs could have effectively supported the separate elements of needs analysis (Focus), feedback (Learn), coaching (Apply), and impact evaluation (Prove), this case showed how one research approach was linked to a strategic initiative to effectively support the entire Focus, Learn, Apply, and Prove HRD value chain.

Conclusion

Market stability, if it ever existed, is a thing of the past. The world of business today is characterized by frequent and bold competitive plays, shortened cycle times, rapid changes in key technologies, and a breakdown in industry and geographic boundaries. This is an increasing reality for most organizations, and as a result they are adapting new models for defining and structuring their enterprise (D'Aveni, 1994). We are finding that the organizational characteristics created in the industrial age do not work within this hypercompetitive market of the knowledge age and are giving way to alternative ways of delivering superior stakeholder value. HRD research that contributes to the HRD value chain in an integrated way is crucial to organizational success in this environment.

References

Baldwin, T. T., & Ford, J. K. (1988). Transfer of training: A review and directions for future research. *Personnel Psychology, 41*, 63–105.

Baldwin, T. T., & Magjuka, R. J. (1991). Organizational training and signals of importance: Effects of pre-training perceptions on intentions to transfer. *Human Resource Development Quarterly, 2*(1), 25–36.

Copeland, T. E., Koller, T., & Murrin, J. (1990). *Valuation: Measuring and managing the value of companies.* New York: Wiley.

D'Aveni, R. (1994). *Hypercompetition.* New York: Free Press.

Galagan, P. A. (1990). David T.: A CEO's view of training. *Training and Development Journal,* (5), 41–50.

Holton, E. F. (1996). The flawed four-level evaluation model. *Human Resource Development Quarterly, 7*(1), 5–21.

Kirkpatrick, D. (1996). Invited reaction: Reaction to Holton article. *Human Resource Development Quarterly, 7*(1), 23–26.

Leimbach, M. P., & Morical, K. E. (1990, July). Evaluation results: Cost-benefit analysis. *Training and Development Yearbook*. Upper Saddle River, NJ: Prentice Hall.

Poole, M. S. (1991). Procedures for managing meetings: Social and technological innovations. In R. A. Swanson & B. O. Knapp (Eds.), *Innovative meeting management*. Austin, TX: 3M.

Porter, M. (1985). *Competitive advantage*. New York: Free Press.

Ralphs, L. T., & Stephan, E. (1986). HRD in the Fortune 500. *Training and Development Journal*, (10), 69–76.

Robinson, D. G., & Robinson, J. C. (1989). *Training for impact: How to link training to business needs and measure the results*. San Francisco: Jossey-Bass.

Rossett, A. (1992). Analysis of human performance problems. In H. D. Stolovitch & E. J. Keeps (Eds.), *Handbook of human performance technology* (pp. 97–113). San Francisco: Jossey-Bass.

Rouillier, J. Z., & Goldstein, I. L. (1993). The relationship between organizational transfer climate and positive transfer of training. *Human Resource Development Quarterly, 4*(4), 377–390.

Schmidt, F. L., Hunter, J. E., & Pearl, K. (1982). Assessing the economic impact of personnel programs on work-force productivity. *Personnel Psychology, 35,* 473–478.

Sheppeck, M. A., & Cohen, S. L. (1985, November). Put a dollar value on your training programs. *Training and Development Journal,* 39(11), 59–62.

Swanson, R. A., & Gradous, D. B. (1988). *Forecasting the financial benefits of human resource development*. San Francisco: Jossey-Bass.

Swanson, R. A., & Sawzin, S. (1976). *Industrial training research project*. Bowling Green, OH: Bowling Green State University.

Tracey, J. B., Tannenbaum, S. I., & Kavanaugh, M. J. (1995). Applying training skills on the job: The importance of the work environment. *Journal of Applied Psychology,* 80(2), 239–252.

Zingheim, P. K., Ledford, E. L., Jr., & Schuster, J. R. (1996, Spring). Competencies and competency models: Does one size fit all? *ACA Journal,* pp. 56–65.

C H A P T E R

HRD Partnerships for Integrating HRD Research and Practice

Ronald L. Jacobs
Ohio State University

The human resource development (HRD) field depends on research being considered an essential counterpart to practice, not an optional activity when convenient or an extravagance when financially possible. Unfortunately, there are relatively few instances that actually illustrate this point, whether in HRD or some other applied field of study (Leimbach, 1995; Ferris, Barnum, Rosen, Holleran, & Dulebohn, 1995)—that is, practice being profoundly influenced by research and vice versa. HRD scholars and practitioners have long been involved in collaborations with each other, which has generally been a good arrangement for both parties. But to what extent these collaborations have actually affected organizational practice and advanced the field can be seriously questioned. This chapter proposes that integrating HRD research and practice requires that a more equitable approach be taken when scholars and practitioners collaborate with each other.

Specifically, this chapter discusses the need to view HRD collaborations as professional partnerships rather than as service agreements. It also offers guidelines for developing HRD collaborations that emphasize research. Finally, the chapter discusses two major implications that affect scholars and practitioners when viewing HRD collaborations as partnerships. Underlying this chapter is the belief that partnerships are key for integrating HRD research with practice, which in turn should help advance the field and improve organizational effectiveness. These dual goals should have equal priority in partnerships and are the ultimate reasons for engaging in HRD collaborations.

HRD Collaborations as Partnerships

In the past decade, a large number of formal and informal collaborations have been formed between university HRD academic programs and organizations (Jacobs & Held, 1993; Carnevale, Gainer, Villet, & Holland, 1990). These collaborations have occurred within the broader societal impetus encouraging greater cooperation between educational institutions, from the most prestigious universities to local vocational schools, and public and private organizations. The nature of these various collaborations has depended in large part on the nature of the educational institution, such as whether it has a research or a community-service mission, and by the perceived needs of the organizations involved, such as whether they need to seek assistance to solve technical issues, managerial issues, or sometimes both.

The predominant purposes of HRD collaborations include joint research and development (R&D) projects, student internships, meetings for professional development, and special conferences. Regardless of the purpose, HRD collaborations have generally resulted in important gains for HRD academic programs and organizations alike. HRD faculty and students have gained through an increased awareness of real-world problems and have provided ready-made opportunities for doing R&D projects with willing and interested clients. HRD practitioners have gained through easier access to faculty and student expertise and greater ability to address pressing organizational issues through R&D projects, often at a reduced cost to the organization. Many HRD practitioners have also gained from an increased exposure to the university milieu, which typically emphasizes a more scholarly and thoughtful approach to problem solving than what is usually taken in their organizations. Often this awareness is the most lasting benefit realized by some practitioners.

Although good in some respects, most HRD collaborations involving research have failed to influence practice and contribute new knowledge to the field. More often than not, at the end of the project, the scholar feels that, although the study met the needs of the organization, there was insufficient rigor in conducting the study, limiting its usefulness beyond the present situation. In other cases, the practitioner feels that, although the research was intrinsically interesting, the study somehow lost its focus and did not adequately respond to the most pressing issues of interest, limiting the practitioner's ability to use the information in the organization. It is proposed in this chapter that HRD collaborations can successfully meet the lofty expectations of both parties, but only if the collaborations are viewed as professional partnerships rather than as service agreements.

Most HRD collaborations between scholars and practitioners become in effect service agreements simply because no other approach seems appropriate. After all, a service agreement is similar in many respects to a customer-supplier relationship, which is well understood in most organizations. However, a service agreement may not be the best approach where HRD research is concerned. In a service agreement, the practitioner, who may not fully understand how best to use the proposed research, sets the requirements for the research study, which often results in limiting the scholar's opportunity. In turn, as a service provider the scholar tends to follow the organization's wishes, which usually means that the research study should have a relatively quick turnaround time and immediate usefulness and should cover a relatively defined range of research questions (Leimbach & Baldwin, 1997).

HRD cannot advance as a field of practice or as a field of study if organizational partners are not willing to invest in research that goes beyond meeting an immediate short-term service need. Ultimately, the organization will suffer when HRD processes are not able to keep pace with changing business needs. The pressure of immediate results is a seductive short-term trap that results in bigger costs in the future. Organization partners need to be willing to invest in basic HRD research to advance the field as well as in efforts to apply research to current organizational needs. Many times the investment is modest, consisting mostly of time and access to employees for research purposes.

HRD scholars and practitioners should seriously consider these requirements when planning the research, but they also should recognize that it would be detrimental if these points were overemphasized. Instead, it is suggested that depending on the research questions, HRD research might have short- or long-term project time lines; might have immediate or delayed benefits to the organization; and, perhaps most important, might have the prerogative to succeed or fail. Thus, in a service agreement, the balance of emphasis is tilted unnecessarily to the wishes of the practitioner, without due regard given to the research itself.

In contrast, a partnership relationship recognizes that scholars and practitioners enter with their own respective goals for the collaboration and that it is important for the common good to maintain the integrity of those goals. Although the goals may differ, they complement each other. Consider that HRD scholars seek out opportunities to systematically advance the field and help organizations, but they need the practitioners' pragmatic insights on the issues of interest and their access to the settings to do this most effectively. At the same time, HRD practitioners seek to help their organizations with useful information and advance the field, though this desire is often less developed, but they need the scholars' ability to frame questions logically and their knowledge of the research literature. Thus, in a partnership relationship, HRD scholars and practitioners serve each other because they are able to achieve goals together that could not possibly have been achieved alone.

A partnership relationship enables HRD research to be viewed more similarly to other research functions in organizations, which themselves have received renewed attention. Increasingly, it is recognized that although research is inherently a gamble, it can bring back knowledge as a return, which may pay off to the organization. But not taking the risk is clearly more damaging in the long run than the risk of losing the initial research investment. More and more authors have commented that organizations have unnecessarily suffered the consequences of their own past limited views and impatience with research (Smith, 1995). An oft-cited example is that of RCA, which, according to some observers, began to dissemble as a major U.S. organization due to senior management's lack of patience in sponsoring the additional research necessary to develop consumer products from the liquid crystal display in the late 1960s, which their own research group had invented. Eventually, RCA allowed others access to the LCD technology, especially the Japanese company Sharp. This resulted in an entirely new generation of consumer products, a fact that was not apparent to anyone at first. Is HRD research any different?

Clearly, there has been a high cost of impatience in organizations when technological research is concerned. What is often less clear, but can be equally damaging to organizations, is the high cost of impatience when HRD research is concerned. HRD research cannot be expected to develop new technologies such as the LCD. But HRD research does develop processes and methodologies that can be expected to significantly help influence the success of those technologies, once developed. For example, the Japanese embraced total quality management when American management was not interested, and they used it to gain a competitive advantage over American products. Even the most elegant technological design remains subject to the broad spectrum of human competence that goes along with developing, producing, and bringing innovations to the marketplace. Simply put, there is no substitute for doing quality research when organizations require practical information.

Guidelines for HRD Collaborations as Partnerships

This chapter makes the point that HRD collaborations emphasizing research should be based on a partnership relationship rather than a service agreement. In truth, rather than being an absolute, a partnership relationship more often than not represents a process goal toward which HRD practitioners and scholars can strive together. Thus, to what extent any one HRD collaboration can be considered a partnership relationship is often a matter of degree. However, HRD collaborations should be developed and maintained according to proven guidelines, which should also help determine whether a partnership relationship is even possible. After all, not all HRD scholars and practitioners may be able to form successful partnership relationships with each other.

Successful partnership relationships should be developed according to the following guidelines:

1. Expect research to be a part of all HRD collaborations.
2. Derive research questions from practice.
3. Determine the use of the research up front.
4. Make HRD collaborations a formal process.
5. Seek long-term HRD collaborations.

1. *Expect research to be a part of all HRD collaborations.* Research is rarely the primary goal of HRD collaborations. In fact, most HRD collaborations focus more on achieving product development goals, such as developing a training program, than on research goals. Regardless of the initial goals, however, HRD collaborations should be automatically viewed as potential opportunities to conduct research. Further, organizations should expect that part of each research collaboration should have as its purpose the advancement of HRD as a field. Thus, the first guideline for scholars and practitioners is that they should at least expect research to be considered as a part of the collaboration, if it is not already. Obviously, it may not be possible for research to be part of every HRD collaboration. However, it may be possible for research to be part of more HRD collaborations than what is often first believed. Indeed, determining the possibility of doing

research likely depends on the prevailing view of research and practice.

Previously, I introduced *partnership research* as a means to integrate HRD research and practice (Jacobs, 1996). Partnership research is simply defined as the process of generating new knowledge through practice. Partnership research suggests that integrating HRD research and practice is best accomplished when the two activities are woven together as much as possible, often both activities occurring at the same time. As an applied field, HRD draws its most enduring principles from a combination of theory and practice. Far too often, however, research is considered a separate entity from practice, limiting the ability of the resulting theory to make substantive contributions to the practice.

2. *Derive research questions from practice.* Another guideline for developing and maintaining successful partnership relationships is that HRD scholars and practitioners should together derive the research problems from practice. This guideline differs from most research approaches, which suggest that scholars should come up with an idea first, go to the literature to confirm whether the idea is in fact worth pursuing further, and then seek out a setting in which to conduct the study (Pace, Smith, & Mills, 1991). Although often an effective approach, this usually places a sizable distance between the research problem and the practice setting, making it difficult to see how the scholar and practitioner could maintain a partnership relationship under those conditions. Deriving the research problem from practice assumes that potential problems may well exist within the setting, which might be of common interest and deserve further consideration (Lawler, Mohrman, Mohrman, Ledford, & Cummings, 1985). Then the research problem is confirmed and further refined through a review of the relevant literature. However,

the original source for identifying the research problem remains practice.

Although different from most other research approaches, deriving research problems from practice still requires that problem statements be constructed from the research questions. Generating research questions such as the following often helps frame the research study: What individual characteristics affect team performance? Which training method will provide the greatest financial benefits? Which team structure is preferable to employees? Is the management development system responsive to the strategic needs of the organization? But in themselves, these questions are not sufficient to guide the research study. Problem statements are typically constructed using a syllogistic format, which includes a principal proposition, an interacting proposition, and a speculative proposition. In combination, these propositional statements form the conceptual boundaries of the study.

3. *Determine the use of the research up front.* The third guideline is that it should be determined up front how the research will be used by each partner. This helps clarify the motivations and expectations upon entering the collaboration, reducing the possibility that one party or the other will be unduly disappointed at the end. Agreement should be reached on how the research will be used both to advance HRD as a field and to meet the organization's needs. Stating how the research will be used also reaffirms the value of the research activity, especially for the practitioner, who may not at first see its broader true value and application. It also provides an opportunity to clearly define whether the project is a service agreement driven by the practitioner's objectives or a research partnership with balanced research and service objectives.

Logically, HRD scholars and practitioners differ in the way they will use the research. HRD scholars generally want to use the research to publish reports such as theses and dissertations, make presentations at professional conferences, and submit manuscripts to scholarly journals. They draw out the generalizable aspects of the research and then communicate this information to an external audience composed of other scholars and practitioners.

Although many practitioners participate in these activities as coauthors or copresenters and appreciate the attention that it brings to them, they are more interested in using the research for other purposes: to write summary memos to senior management, prepare short reports for limited distribution, and make presentations to a variety of internal audiences. In other words, the research is used in the practitioner's organization to help others become more aware of specific issues, make more effective decisions, solve problems more accurately, and support whatever actions are required to improve the organization in some way.

4. *Make HRD collaborations a formal process*. As with any partnership, HRD collaborations are composed of individuals who often have differing sets of assumptions, personal goals, and professional pressures. Conflicts and misunderstandings are bound to occur, even under the best of circumstances. Therefore, the fourth guideline is to formalize HRD collaborations as much as possible. Contracts are a major means of doing so. Scholars and practitioners should negotiate a mutually agreeable contract for each project, which describes the project goals, expectations of each partner during the project, products to be delivered, project time line, project costs, and a statement regarding renegotiation. The contract may also include a statement that the project represents a collaboration intended to be a partnership relationship to achieve the goals of both the researcher and the practitioner.

Although contracts are helpful in many respects, they in themselves cannot possibly address all the issues that arise within HRD collaborations. Other formal activities include regularly scheduled project meetings and interim reporting sessions. In addition, it is incumbent upon both scholar and practitioner, regardless of how good their relationship, to speak out when the collaboration is not working as expected. For example, if the HRD practitioner is heard among a group of managers to downplay the value of the research, this might be interpreted as the weakening of the organization's commitment to the research or the practitioner simply yielding to the uninformed skepticism of others. In such a situation, which could occur with either the scholar or the practitioner, there should be an open discussion of the matter. In many respects, striving for a partnership relationship is a continuous learning experience for both scholars and practitioners.

5. *Seek long-term HRD collaborations*. The final guideline is for scholars and practitioners alike to seek long-term HRD collaborations with each other. A long-term HRD collaboration is loosely defined as one in which more than one project, or even a series of projects, is expected to occur as part of the collaboration. Long-term collaborations are not possible in all instances, but when possible they are strongly encouraged. In general, long-term HRD collaborations provide the extended time and repeated contacts necessary to help build mutual trust and respect, attributes essential for developing a true partnership. For instance, many practitioners initially question the scholar's role in the HRD profession until they themselves have become involved in a partnership research project of their own.

More specifically, long-term HRD collaborations enable scholars to better understand the organization and its particular situation. It may also enable the scholar to plan a series of related research studies that also meet the information needs of the organization. Long-term HRD collaborations enable practitioners to better understand the research process and gain experience in performing some of the technical aspects of doing research, such as selecting and interpreting statistics or analyzing qualitative data from interviews. Generally the greatest contributions to advancing HRD as a field as well as the organizations that employ HRD processes emerge from long-term collaborations.

Implications of
HRD Collaborations as Partnerships

Numerous implications arise when HRD collaborations become more like partnership relationships than service agreements. However, two major implications are especially important in this discussion: (1) HRD practitioners should know more about research and (2) HRD scholars should know more about practice.

1. *HRD practitioners should know research.* The requirements for entering the HRD profession have increased dramatically in the past decade. More and more organizations understand the value of having HRD staff members with advanced degrees in the field. Nevertheless, there is a continuing need for HRD practitioners to know more about research—not that they should know more about what the research says on any one topic, such as the effects of feedback or the comparative financial benefits of particular training approaches (most HRD graduate programs provide adequate reviews of the pertinent HRD literature) but rather that they should know more about how to use research as a means to improve practice. Practitioners who understand the research process also understand that even modest investments in long-term HRD research can yield enormous benefits if done on a continuous basis. They also understand that the research process necessarily involves projects without immediate payoff or application but that lead to later projects that do have immediate application.

If HRD practitioners are to become successful partners with scholars, then they need more knowledge about specific topics such as engaging in HRD collaborations with scholars and conducting partnership research studies. At present, such knowledge is often lacking even among the most enlightened HRD practitioners. Further, it is suggested that HRD scholars have a professional stake in helping to address this implication. Through their own efforts as instructors and advisors, HRD scholars can bring about the needed changes in how research is viewed and, at the same time, affect the quality of their own future collaborations with HRD practitioners.

2. *HRD scholars should know practice.* HRD collaborations as partnerships also have important implications for scholars. It is suggested that scholars should know practice better or at least seek to become accomplished practitioners themselves if they are not already. This implication arises from the nature of most HRD collaborations: they emphasize the achievement of product development goals, from which the research problems are derived. Paradoxically, if HRD scholars are not effective as practitioners, at least to some extent, then their own research opportunities will necessarily become more limited. In effect, HRD scholars must view their own personal research agendas as being linked with the various practice opportunities that they take on.

This implication may not fit with the desires or personalities of all HRD scholars. In some instances, it may mean that scholars must relinquish some control of their own research agendas and preferred ways of doing research. For instance, whereas partnership research in itself does not necessarily show preference for any one research method or design, it may in fact preclude using certain types of research designs that demand greater control and manipulation of the setting. Yet such techniques are not used for every research study, and when they are, additional planning would be called for to anticipate their use.

Conclusion

This chapter proposes that to achieve the dual goals of advancing the field and improving organizations, HRD collaborations should be viewed as partnerships rather than as service agreements. This proposal may appeal to many HRD scholars and practitioners in the abstract, but how to actually accomplish such a transformation remains a challenge for many of us. After all, HRD collaborations exist within a larger organizational context, which determines in no small part how the scholar and practitioner will work together. However, it remains the responsibility of HRD scholars and practitioners working together to provide the best possible information to organizations and the field. A heightened commitment is needed by both to conduct research that advances the field as well as research projects that meet organizational needs. Otherwise, gains in influence by the HRD profession in the recent past are not likely to be carried into the future.

References

Carnevale, A., Gainer, L. J., Villet, J., & Holland, S. L. (1990). *Training partnerships: Linking employers and providers.* Alexandria, VA: American Society for Training and Development.

Ferris, G. R., Barnum, D. T., Rosen, S. D., Holleran, L. P., & Dulebohn, J. H. (1995). Toward business-industry partnerships in human resource management: Integration of science and practice. In G. R. Ferris, S. D. Rosen, & D. T. Barnum (Eds.), *Handbook of human resource management* (pp. 1–13). Cambridge, MA: Blackwell.

Jacobs, R. L. (1996). Partnership research: Pulling rabbits from hats. *Human Resource Development Quarterly, 7*(2), 117–119.

Jacobs, R. L., & Held, M. (1993). *Rethinking the Business-Industry Consortium: Proposing a new direction.* Unpublished evaluation report, graduate program in Human Resource Development, Ohio State University at Columbus.

Lawler, E. E., Mohrman, A. M., Mohrman, S. A., Ledford, G. E., & Cummings, T. G. (1985). *Doing research that is useful for theory and practice.* San Francisco: Jossey-Bass.

Leimbach, M. (1995). Research: The thin blue line between rigor and reality. In E. Holton (Ed.), *Academy of Human Resource Development: 1995 Annual Conference Proceedings.* Austin, TX: Academy of Human Resource Development.

Leimbach, M. P., & Baldwin, T. T. (1997). How research contributes to the HRD value chain. In R. A. Swanson and E. F. Holton III (Eds.), *Human resource development research handbook.* San Francisco: Berrett-Koehler.

Pace, R. W., Smith, P. C., & Mills, G. E. (1991). *Human resource development: The field.* Upper Saddle River, NJ: Prentice Hall.

Smith, H. (1995). *Rethinking America: Innovative strategies and partnerships in business and education.* New York: Avon Books.

PART TWO

Ways of Doing
Practical Research

CHAPTER 4

Quantitative Research Methods

Elwood F. Holton III
Louisiana State University

Michael F. Burnett
Louisiana State University

Quantitative methods and the scientific method are the foundation of modern science. This approach to research usually starts with specific theory, either proposed or previously developed, which leads to specific hypotheses that are then measured quantitatively and rigorously analyzed and evaluated according to established research procedures. This approach has a rich tradition and has contributed a substantial portion of the knowledge in human resource development (HRD).

This chapter attempts to demystify the quantitative research process and tools that HRD researchers use. It is not a statistics chapter, though it includes discussion of statistical tools. Rather, its purpose is to give you an overview of quantitative research so you can do two things: 1) read research reports more easily and 2) understand choices made by researchers. It is not complete in describing every statistical tool nor in explaining all the nuances of the various methods. Instead, it should provide a frame of reference to help you feel comfortable in the world of quantitative research.

Strengths of Quantitative Research

HRD researchers use both quantitative and qualitative methods (see Chapter Five, "Qualitative Research Methods"). The basic premise of this book is that both research methods are valuable; in fact they are often quite powerful when used together. Researchers collect data for two basic reasons: to better understand phenomena in a specific group being studied and to make inferences about broader groups beyond those being studied. We will say more about these two concepts later. Quantitative techniques are particularly strong at studying large groups of people and applying generalizations from the sample being studied to broader groups beyond that sample. Qualitative methods, on the other hand, are particularly strong at attaining deep and detailed understandings about a specific group or sample but at the expense of generalizability. Each approach has unique strengths and weaknesses; each is valuable depending on the purpose of the research.

Quality Considerations

The area of greatest misunderstanding between researchers and practitioners about quantitative methods probably lies in issues of quality. It is common for researchers to want to use procedures that seem like excessive work to practitioners. Researchers and their methods then may be labeled unrealistic or ivory tower. As discussed earlier in this book, research has a different purpose than practice. Whereas "seat of the pants" methods might be quite acceptable for certain organizational decisions, research necessarily has a higher quality standard.

How much quality is needed? Most research is not conducted solely for the purpose of understanding a single event occurring for a single group of people; it is almost always used to draw some conclusions beyond the group being studied. For example, if evaluation research is conducted on the first two training programs offered in a new supervisory training program, it will likely be used to make decisions about how well it will work for other groups of supervisors who will complete the program. Researchers call this *generalization*. Depending upon the level of generalization, the research procedures may need to be either complex or simple. If all we care about is understanding the results for these two groups of supervisors—and nothing more—the procedures will be much simpler than if we want to know if the results will likely be the same for any group of supervisors from any of the organization's facilities in the United States. The procedures will be even more complex if we want to know if it will work at any of the company's facilities in the world. They will grow even more complex if the organization conducting the research is a consulting firm that wants to know if the program will work not only anywhere in the world but also with any type of company.

The other parameter that affects the complexity of the procedures is the *degree of certainty* required from the research. If the stakes are very high (e.g., a huge amount of money is being invested in the intervention, lives depend on the outcomes, etc.), then the researchers need to have a high degree of certainty that there is no error in the research results. This will require very strict and complex research procedures. On the other hand, if the stakes are much lower, then a lower degree of certainty may be acceptable.

Researchers are concerned about breadth of generalization and the degree of certainty they have in the findings because the implications of the research cannot exceed the scope of what was studied and how it was studied. However, practitioners under pressure to make quick business decisions often want only narrow generalization and will accept lower degrees of certainty. This usually presents a challenge when researchers and practitioners create partnerships because their goals may differ (see Chapter Three for a complete discussion of research partnerships). What is most important in partnerships is that both parties negotiate and agree to the goal of the research. If the goal is simply to provide one organization with the data it needs to make appropriate decisions, then the organization should make that clear, and the researchers, if they choose to accept the project, must design the research procedures accordingly. However, if the organization also wants to contribute to the growth of the HRD profession through research, then the organization should be prepared to accept more complex research procedures than necessary for its own short-term needs.

Overview of Quantitative Research Process

The quantitative research process can be viewed as a five-step process as outlined below and detailed in the follow-up sections:

1. Determining basic questions to be answered by study
2. Determining participants in the study (population and sample)

3. Selecting the methods needed to answer questions
   a. Variables
   b. Measures of the variables
   c. Constructing measurement tools
   d. Building valid scales
   e. Overall design
4. Selecting analysis tools
5. Understanding and interpreting the results

Determining Basic Questions

Formulating the research questions is perhaps the most important step in any research effort. Without a clear understanding of the outcomes expected from the study and the questions to be answered, there is a high likelihood of error.

Quantitative research is generally either experimental, quasi-experimental, correlational, or descriptive. In experimental research, researchers deliberately set out to create specific conditions to test a theory or proposition. Specific hypotheses are created from theory that are then tested by the experiment. For example, you might randomly select and assign employees to two different types of training methods to see if it affects their performance because we believe training method will affect the outcomes. In experimental research, the researcher controls many of the factors that influence the phenomenon of interest in order to isolate relationships between conditions or behaviors we can change and the outcomes that result.

Nonexperimental research, on the other hand, uses existing situations in the field to study phenomena. It is used when it is impractical to conduct a true experiment, to study more variables than can be controlled in an experiment, or when there is a need

Quasi

for descriptive quantitative data. However, the researcher does not take control of variables as in experimental research. For example, through quasi-experimental research you could also test the proposition that training method affects performance, but you would be using existing training classes and methods rather than deliberately creating the training and training situation. Quasi-experimental research to test theory is a very common type of quantitative research in HRD because of the difficulties in creating true experiments in organizational settings.

The other forms of nonexperimental research can be thought of as causal-comparative, correlational, and descriptive (survey) research (Ary, Jacobs, & Razavieh, 1996): *causal-comparative research* is similar to an experiment except that the researcher does not manipulate the variable(s) being studied. Researchers attempt to find subjects who differ on some variable of interest and then attempt to discover other variables that explain the difference in order to infer causality. *Correlational research* seeks to determine relationships among two or more variables without necessarily inferring causality. Both causal-comparative and correlational research generally begin with hypotheses generated from theory. *Descriptive research* uses surveys to gather information about people, groups, organizations, etc. Its purpose is simply to describe characteristics of the domain.

An overlooked role for quantitative methods is in discovering theory (McCall & Bobko, 1990). Quantitative research can also be exploratory—that is, used to discover relationships, interpretations, and characteristics of subjects that suggest new theory and define new problems. When used for this purpose, research questions are used instead of specific hypotheses. Thus, a "loose-tight" approach to the application of quantitative methods is advocated, depending on the overriding goal of the research. If the purpose is to test theory for broad generalization to many audiences, then rigorous application of quantitative methodology is needed. If the purpose is to discover theoretical propositions or define problems in need of theory, then looser application of these techniques is perfectly acceptable. It is in the latter arena that quantitative and qualitative techniques are most similar.

Determining Participants

One of the real advantages of quantitative methods is their ability to use smaller groups of people to make inferences about larger groups that would be prohibitively expensive to study. For example, imagine the cost of establishing the effectiveness of a particular supervisory development tool if researchers had to study every supervisor in the company throughout the country!

The research term for all the supervisors in this example is the *population*. In any study, there is usually a population—the larger group to which the results from the research being conducted are believed to be applicable. It is very important to define the degree to which the results will need to be generalized beyond the study because that is one of the factors that determines the rigor of the study. Statistical tools let us use smaller groups, called *samples*, in our studies. However, in order to make generalizations from the study, researchers prefer to choose that sample randomly. By doing so, they can have much greater confidence that their findings are not due to some special characteristic of the sample but rather are truly representative of the whole population.

Obtaining random samples is often a difficult issue in HRD research because much research is conducted inside organizations. Sometimes organizational conditions such as production schedules or the requirement to work with intact groups simply will not accommodate gathering random samples. Other times, ethical issues preclude it, such as giving one group of employees tools that enable them to perform better than their peers. Sometimes the nature of the intervention itself precludes it, such as when developing teams. Other times, economics limit it because it simply is not good business. Despite these limitations, HRD researchers need sites willing to accommodate strict sampling procedures to advance the field.

Selecting Methods

Once the researcher has identified the research questions and the participants in the study, the specific methods to be used in the study can be determined. These include identifying the variables, measures, and research design.

Variables

Variables are the phenomena that vary depending on the conditions affecting them. Researchers talk about two types of variables: *dependent* and *independent*. A dependent variable is the variable that is the object of the study or the studied outcome. Examples might include learning, job performance, or company market share. An independent variable is a measure that is believed to be related in some way to the dependent variable. For example, supervisor support for training (independent variable) is widely believed to influence the use of training on the job (dependent variable). A further extension here would be that the use of training (independent variable) is widely believed to influence the quantity and quality of work (dependent variable).

Measures of the Variables

Both independent and dependent variables can be measured by either *categorical* data, *continuous* data, or *ordinal* data. Categorical, or nominal, data come from measures that have no inherent numeric value; they are simply categories such as gender, department, teaching method used, etc. Although researchers may assign a coding number to these categories for ease of computer analysis (e.g., female = 1, male = 2), the number has no real meaning. The codes could have just as easily been "A" or "B."

Continuous, or interval, data, on the other hand, are data that have an intrinsic numeric value. Examples might include a person's salary, output in units, scrap or rework rates, performance rating, test score, or rating in a simulation exercise. Ordinal, or rank order, data is less descriptive than interval data. For example, five people could be rank ordered in height as 1, 2, and 3, which lets you know that 1 is taller than 2 (one rank order position apart). But to indicate that the tallest person is 76", the second tallest is 66", and the third tallest is 65" is much more descriptive of the true heights and differences. It is important to never collect ordinal data when interval data can be just as easily obtained. One common example of HRD research data is that obtained from survey data asking for responses on a Likert scale (1–4; 1–5; 1–9). Statistically, this data can be handled as continuous data.

The result is that measures can be viewed in a 3 x 2 matrix. As shown in Figure 4.1, independent variable data may be either categorical, continuous (interval), or ordinal. Similarly, dependent variable data may be either categorical or continuous.

Constructing Measurement Tools. So far, we have been talking about measures as if they were easy to come by. In fact, a large part of conducting good research is obtaining or building good measures of the variables in a research study. The quality of the research results is as much dependent on good measures as anything else researchers do. The best analysis in the world cannot compensate for poorly constructed measures.

	Independent Variable	Dependent Variable
Categorical		
Continuous (Interval)		
Ordinal		

Figure 4.1. Types of Variables

There are four basic types of measures used in HRD studies:

1. *Observational measures*—measures recorded by an observer. Performance ratings, 360–degree feedback, and checklists are examples.
2. *Self-report measures*—a person in the study's own report. Examples include a trainee's report of use of training on the job or knowledge gained.
3. *Objective measures*—measures taken by instruments or highly accurate measuring devices. Examples might include cost data, quality measures from equipment, or knowledge tests.
4. *Estimates*—estimates of measures, usually by subject matter experts.

To evaluate any of these, two concepts have to be clear: *validity* and *reliability*. Measures are said to be valid if they measure what they are supposed to measure. Thus, self-report measures of performance on the job tend to not be very valid because people tend to overrate themselves. A reliable measure is one that yields consistent results. A measure can be very reliable (consistent) but not valid (measure inaccurately or the wrong thing). For example, self ratings are very often reliable but not valid.

These concepts are significant for practitioners. For one thing, you will see both of them discussed at length in most research articles. Also, before you accept research findings, you want to be sure valid and reliable measures are used. If you are conducting or sponsoring research in your organization, you want to be sure that you have valid and reliable measures so the conclusions you report to your boss are the correct ones. Finally, if you create research partnerships, you may spend considerable time discussing these concepts and need resources devoted to developing valid and reliable measures.

There are three common types of validity. *Content validity*, the minimum requirement for acceptable research, means that the content of your measure matches the content of what you are trying to measure. For example, a performance rating instrument is content valid if the items on the instrument match what is really required to do the job. This is usually established by subject matter experts and is done logically, not statistically.

Criterion validity, on the other hand, asks whether the measure really predicts the dependent variable it is supposed to predict. Thus, we would expect our performance rating instrument to be able to predict, or distinguish, high performers from low performers. If we find that successful people in an organization have widely varying scores on the performance rating instrument, then the instrument would not have good criterion validity. An instrument could have good content validity (appear to have the right content) but not good criterion validity, probably because important things were left off the instrument.

The third type of validity is *construct validity*. A construct is something that cannot be directly observed or measured. Job commitment or motivation are examples. We can measure behaviors that are believed to represent commitment or motivation, but we cannot measure them directly as we can scrap or sales. Because indirect measures have to be used, researchers have to establish that what they actually measure is really the construct they believe they are measuring. This is usually done by comparing the measure to similar or related measures.

Building Valid Scales. Some measures are obtained from single objective and numerical data. For example, the number of sales made in a day, scrap rate, or age are all single numbers that are relatively easy to obtain. Other variables need to be measured more indirectly. Examples might include supervisor performance rating, personality type, job commitment, or motivation. In these cases, researchers develop *scales* that consist of multiple questions that are mathematically grouped together to measure a variable.

The development and testing of valid measurement scales is a special type of research. Researchers use a tool called *factor analysis* to build valid measurement scales. In this approach, researchers generate items for instruments, usually with the help of subject matter experts. A group of people then respond to the instrument, and factor analysis is used to look at the relationship between the items. By looking at the results, researchers can tell which items seem to be measuring the same thing so they can then be grouped into scales for further analysis.

Overall Design. The design of an experimental or quasi-experimental research study refers to the way in which the data will be collected. There are really three basic design decisions to be made, though they are often combined into many different variations. The three design tools are (1) pre-tests, (2) control groups, and (3) time series. Each of them enables researchers to answer additional questions from the data.

Question 1: Is what we are observing now a change? Suppose we have measured individual performance after learning and find that it is at acceptable levels. Was the money invested in learning worthwhile? It could have been completely wasted because performance was just fine before the learning! The only way to be sure is to use a *pre-test*. A pre-test does not necessarily mean a traditional classroom test; it simply means taking a measure of whatever we are interested in before our intervention. These are sometime referred to as baseline measures.

Question 2: Is a change due to our intervention? Continuing the above example, suppose that we include a pre-test and we find that yes, performance did go up and our statistics tell us that it was a significant change. Can we now say that our learning intervention worked? No, not yet. It could have been that everyone got a raise or a new supervisor at the same time as the intervention. If we want to control for the possibility that something else caused what we observe, we have to use a *control group*. A control group is nothing more than a group that is as close as possible to being the same as the people we are studying but who do not get the learning intervention. The idea is that anything else that might affect our study group will affect the control group similarly. We won't know what it is, but we will know that the difference between the control group and our study group should be just the learning. Of course, it is often hard work to get a control group that is the "same" as our study group. Sometimes we have a control group that is almost the same (trainees who come on Wednesday versus those coming in two weeks) or similar but not identical (two plant sites). In HRD research, it is often hard to get a true control group, so researchers spend a great deal of time measuring and establishing the degree to which two groups are similar.

Question 3: Are the changes consistent over time? If your work performance is measured today, will it be the same tomorrow, or one month from now, given the same task? Probably not. Often researchers are not satisfied with just one measure before or after the learning. Measures taken at a single point in time tend to be somewhat suspect. When measuring performance, for example, a person could be ill or simply having a bad day. If we took a measure once a week and averaged them, it might be more valid. Or it might be easy to implement a new process when we measure performance one month after learning it. However, will the employee continue to do it three months or six months after the learning? These are all applications for *time series* or repeated measures.

Researchers combine these three basic building blocks to create many different designs for research, depending on the purpose of the research: control group with pre-test, single group pre-test with time series, etc. By knowing these three basic components, you can understand just about any design.

❖

Selecting Analysis Tools

There are many statistical analysis tools. This section will orient you to the most common analysis tools that you will encounter when reading research or working with researchers.

Beginning researchers often equate certain analytical tools with the different types of research studies. Although there is some relationship, data analysis tools can be used for different purposes and in different types of studies. For example, analysis of variance might be used in an experimental or nonexperimental study. Insights into the decisions researchers make about quantitative analysis tools can be gained by understanding two things: 1) what the basic questions being asked by the researcher are and 2) whether the data from the measures being used are continuous *(interval)*, ordinal, or categorical.

It is convenient to think of quantitative tools as being used to answer one of five core questions:

1. *Description:* What are the characteristics of some group or groups of people?
2. *Comparison of groups:* Are two or more groups the same or different on some characteristic?
3. *Association:* Are two variables related and, if so, what is the strength of their relationship?
4. *Prediction:* Can measures be used to predict something in the future?
5. *Explanation:* Given some outcome or phenomena, why does it occur?

Purpose: Describe. At least part of most studies is simply to describe certain aspects of a group of people. If it is the entire purpose, the study is called a *descriptive study.* Consider, for example, a researcher who conducts a mail survey to investigate training needs of HRD professionals in a particular area. The survey might include certain demographics such as age, gender, and type of company. These data are categorical data. They would be analyzed using *frequencies,* which are simply percentages. Along with this data, the researcher might list six different training needs and ask people responding to indicate on a scale of 1 to 5 how badly they need each training program. These responses are continuous data, so the researcher would first report simple *means* or averages to describe the average level of need. These two tools are the basic measures used to describe a group of people.

Suppose that the mean response to the need for training in instructional design is 3.3. We know that the average level of need is a little above the midpoint, but it raises another question: Was everyone about at that level, or did some people answer 5 and others 1? Researchers look at another measure called a *standard deviation* to answer this question. A standard deviation tells you how widely the responses vary around the mean. In this case, a standard deviation of .2 would indicate that everyone responded pretty close to 3.3, whereas a standard deviation of .8 would indicate that answers varied much more widely. It turns out that, on average, about 66 percent of the responses will be within ± 1 standard deviation of a mean, and 95 percent will be within ± 2 standard deviations.

Purpose: Compare. Once people see the means, they inevitably want to compare them between groups. For example, we might want to compare the mean responses of males and females to the above question. If males had an average response of 3.2 and females 3.25, we might be satisfied to "eyeball it" and say there is no real difference. Similarly, if males responded 3.2 and females 4.2, we would be pretty confident there is a real difference. But suppose males had an average response of 3.2 and females an average response of 3.5. Is that difference a real difference, or close enough to say they are about the same? Researchers use a statistical tool called a *t-test* to compare means between two groups. This is simply a tool to indicate whether the difference is likely to be a "real" difference.

Now suppose that instead of comparing the means between males and females we want to compare the means between three groups such as those in three different departments. For example, suppose that department A's mean response is 3.2, department B's is 3.5, and department C's is 3.7.

A t-test will not work because it only works with two groups, so instead researchers use a technique called *analysis of variance*, or more commonly ANOVA. This technique tells you the same thing as a t-test but with more than two groups. If the result is "significant" (a statistical concept explained later in this chapter), the researcher knows that there is a difference among the three scores.

In this case, the dependent variable is the mean response that is continuous. The independent variable is the department because we are asking if department predicts the mean response. It is a categorical variable. Analysis of variance always has categorical independent and continuous dependent variables. If the independent variable is continuous, you have to use regression, which is explained later in this chapter. Analysis of variance is a very commonly used technique in HRD. Comparisons among different teaching methods, departments, or types of interventions would all require ANOVA as an analysis tool.

You will see other variations of ANOVA. One is called *factorial ANOVA*, which simply means that instead of one category as an independent variable, there are two or more. This is quite common because there are usually at least two categorical variables involved as independent variables in a study. For example, when comparing three different training methods we might also include job level as another independent variable because it could affect trainees' response to the teaching method. *Analysis of covariance (ANCOVA)* is a close cousin that allows for one of the independent variables to be continuous. For example, we might use ANCOVA if we were comparing three departments using two different teaching methods in each one and wanted to include age (a continuous variable) in the study. *Multiple analysis of variance (MANOVA)* is used if there is more than one dependent variable. All help us answer the same question: Are there differences among groups or categories?

Purpose: Association. Suppose now that instead of looking at different groups, we are interested in the association between measures. For example, suppose that I want to know if salary level is associated with test scores. Note that the question is not whether one *causes* the other but whether there is some association between them. The tool researchers use to investigate association between two measures is *correlation*. A correlation always

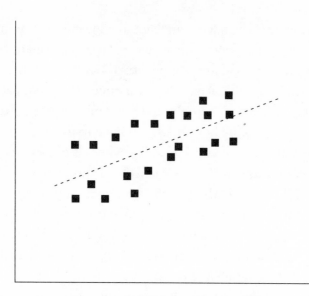

Figure 4.2. High Positive Correlation

ranges from −1.0 to +1.0 and tells us two things: the direction of the association and the strength of the association. The sign of the correlation tells us if it is a positive association (e.g., when one variable goes up, the other one does too) or negative (when one goes up, the other one goes down). The strength of the association is indicated by the actual number and how close it is to ±1, which is a perfect correlation. Suppose the correlation between salary and test scores is −.50. This tells you that people with higher salaries tend to score lower on the tests (a negative relationship) and that the association is moderately strong (.5 is half way between 0 and 1). Figure 4.2 shows a high positive correlation; Figure 4.3 gives an example of a low negative correlation.

Correlations do not tell us anything about causation, which is a mistake frequently made when interpreting them. In our example, does the −.50 correlation mean that making more money makes you less smart so you do worse on tests? Or, conversely,

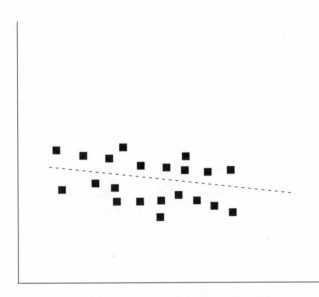

Figure 4.3. Low Negative Correlation

does it mean that doing well on tests causes you to make less money? No to both of them. There is some other variable (time available to study, relevance of the material to their job, etc.) that probably explains the relationship. Correlation only tells us that a relationship exists, not whether it is causal.

The correlation just described can only be used with two continuous variables. There are other correlations that can be used with categorical variables, though they are less common in HRD research. Some you might see include *Spearman's Rho*, the *Phi coefficient*, and the *point-biserial correlation*. They do the same thing as the Pearson correlation (described above) but with different types of categorical data.

Purpose: Prediction. The logical extension of correlation is to try to predict some dependent variable, such as performance or learning. Instead of examining simple correlations between two variables, the next step researchers take is to combine multiple independent variables to examine their joint association with the dependent variable. The analysis tool they use is *regression*, or more specifically *multiple regression*, when there is more than one independent variable. It turns out that the output from this analysis is an equation that can be used to predict the outcome given a new set of values for the independent variables. For example, we might investigate whether a combination of measures of job commitment, supervisor support for training, and salary level could be used to predict test scores, and if so, how strong that relationship is. This is an example of multiple regression analysis.

Regression analysis is typically used when most of the independent variables are continuous variables, although techniques exist (called *dummy coding*) that allow some categorical variables to be included. Actually, correlation, analysis of variance, and regression are essentially the same mathematical process, but analysis of variance works best when most of the independent variables are categorical, whereas correlation and regression work best when most of them are continuous.

A note of caution: prediction still does not imply a causal relationship. That is, we might have measures that successfully predict a dependent variable but do not cause it. A simple example illustrates this. We can probably predict salary level by measuring square footage of people's houses, the neighborhood they live in, and the price of the cars they own, but these factors do not cause the salary. They are merely associated with it and will probably mathematically predict it.

Purpose: Explain. The highest level of research is explanation, or establishing causality. This is very demanding and often costly research. Research for the purpose of explanation seeks to understand why some phenomena occur. If we want to intervene and affect outcomes, it is not enough to say that it does or that it can be predicted. We need to explain *why* something occurs.

Continuing the example about house size and salary, we have no idea from that research what factors lead to higher salaries, so we have no idea how to help young people develop their careers. If we are in advertising and simply want to know to whom our ads should be mailed, that doesn't matter, but if we are educators wanting to help young people, it matters a great deal.

The tools we have discussed can be used to suggest possible causal relationships, but researchers seeking explanations have to use much more sophisticated tools. The best approach to determine causality is to conduct experimental research. Non-experimental research can be used to strongly infer causal relationships if tools such as structural equation modeling or path analysis are used. Hierarchical regression is a more simple but useful approach. These tools typically require larger samples and more rigorous methodology than regression analysis.

Research for explanation is an area in which practitioners tend to be less tolerant when partnering with researchers. In business, intuitive understandings are often sufficient for decisions. Thus, when faced with the time and cost demands for explanatory research, practitioners tend to not want to support it. However, to advance the field of HRD and to provide solid theoretical foundations for practice, it is essential that organizations invest in explanatory research. Researchers need field sites that understand the long-term value of this research and are willing to do more than is required for their immediate decision-making purposes.

Understanding and Interpreting the Results

The concept of *significance* is critical in understanding and interpreting results. Research never really "proves" anything. What researchers do is use elaborate sets of procedures to reduce the probability of an error to such an extent that they can be extremely confident that the answer is the real answer and not just a fluke occurrence. That is why researchers talk and write a lot about "*p*" values. When reading research studies, you will see many references to "p ≤ .05" or "p ≤ .01." This is the standard way researchers examine results. P values mean that the researcher is 95 percent or 99 percent confident that whatever was found is real and not just a chance occurrence. By convention, "p ≤ .05" is the level at which a finding is considered *significant*. This is a very important concept because findings may look meaningful but not be statistically significant (and vice versa).

For example, suppose that one class has an average test score of 85 percent and another has an average score of 89.3 percent. You would like to know if the one group really learned more than the other. The question that researchers have to answer is whether we can be certain that the difference is "real" or just a chance occurrence. It looks real, but is it? Statistical procedures actually approach this backward by starting with the hypothesis that the difference is really equal to zero and trying to disprove it. If the appropriate test results in "p ≤ .05," this means that there is less than a 5 percent chance that the difference is zero. Said differently, there is a 95 percent chance that the group that had an average test score of 89.2 percent actually learned more than the group with an 85 percent average score.

Conclusion

Although the tools and methodologies available for research continue to expand to embrace new paradigms and approaches, quantitative approaches to research will always remain a core approach to HRD research. Without them, the ability of researchers to provide guidance across multiple organizations and groups of employees would be limited. Together with qualitative tools, they enable research to advance HRD practice.

Reading and understanding quantitative approaches is much like learning a foreign language. At first, the effort can be intimidating and confusing, but with a little persistence and some help translating unfamiliar words, it becomes more clear. With only a basic understanding, most practitioners can become good consumers of HRD research and more effective research partners. It is worth the effort.

References

Ary, D., Jacobs, L. C., & Razavieh, A. (1996). *Introduction to research in education* (5th ed.). Fort Worth, TX: Harcourt Brace.

McCall, M. W., & Bobko, P. (1990). Research methods in the service of discovery. In M. D. Dunnette & L. Hough (Eds.), *Handbook of industrial and organizational psychology* (pp. 381–418). Palo Alto, CA: Consulting Psychologists Press.

Further Reading

Bobko, P. (1995). *Correlation and regression.* New York: McGraw-Hill.

Borg, W. R., & Gall, M. D. (1992). *Educational research* (4th ed.). New York: Longman.

Campbell, D. T., & Stanley, J. C. (1963). *Experimental and quasi-experimental designs for research.* Boston: Houghton Mifflin.

Huck, S. W., & Cormier, W. H. (1996). *Reading statistics and research.* New York: HarperCollins.

Kerlinger, F. N. (1986). *Foundations of behavioral research* (3rd ed.). Austin, TX: Holt, Rinehart and Winston.

C H A P T E R

Qualitative
Research Methods

Barbara L. Swanson
Swanson & Associates, Inc.

Karen E. Watkins
University of Georgia

Victoria J. Marsick
Columbia University

Views differ on the nature of qualitative research. In this chapter, we use the definition offered by Denzin and Lincoln (1994):

> Qualitative research is multimethod in focus, involving an interpretive, naturalistic approach to its subject matter. This means that qualitative researchers study things in their natural settings, attempting to make sense of, or interpret, phenomena in terms of the meanings people bring to them. Qualitative research involves the studied use and collection of a variety of empirical materials: case study, personal experience, introspective, life story, interview, observational, historical, interactive, and visual texts that describe routine and problematic moments and meanings in individuals lives [p. 2].

We begin this chapter by further examining the nature of qualitative research and when it is most appropriate to use in human resource development (HRD). We then discuss strategies, tools, data collection, and analysis.

Nature of Qualitative Research

Qualitative research is often defined most by what it is not—that is, by the absence of *purely* quantitative methods and analysis—than by what it is. Qualitative research uses methods that speak to quality, that is, nuances, perceptions, viewpoints, meaning, relationships, stories, and dynamic changing perspectives. Beyond that commonality, qualitative research can differ greatly due to the viewpoints the researcher holds about the nature of reality,[1] the purpose of the research, and the professional discipline of the researcher—for example, organization developer, ethnographer, sociologist, policy analyst, or linguist.

Interest in qualitative research has been growing steadily. Many social scientists believe in an objective world where researchers can develop and test hypotheses that yield a body of theory that represents truth. Other social scientists, often referred to as postmodern, question this positivist and postpositivist perspective. They believe that there is no one truth and subscribe to the idea that people co-construct the social and cultural worlds they inhabit.

---

[1]Miles and Huberman (1994) include a graphic overview of qualitative research by R. Tesch that traces some of these different traditions. Some of the more frequently mentioned (and sometimes overlapping) varieties include ethnography, grounded theory, life history, community studies, ethnomethodology, critical theory, semiotics, hermeneutics, phenomenology, cultural studies, and collaborative inquiry.

Quantitative researchers attempt to remain neutral, objective, and apart from the reality they study. They try to create a research environment devoid of extraneous influences or attempt to have them operate equally among groups so that they can isolate key causes, ensure reliability and validity, and strengthen predictive capability of the phenomena being studied. However, qualitative researchers study people and events in their natural environment, because that is the nature of the messy reality with which those researched must contend. Qualitative researchers also recognize that they inevitably play a role in shaping that which they study. They are part of the milieu that is being constructed. Inevitably, they also filter their views through their own life experience.

Qualitative research thus reflects the assertion that there are multiple realities. Some qualitative researchers, called realists, believe that they can collect, describe, and compare these multiple realities to some sort of an objective reality.[2] Others believe that good research can only illuminate these differences. Qualitative researchers also acknowledge and examine their own historically situated perspective as a filter for the discussion of differences.

Pragmatic Value of Qualitative Research

Social scientists turn to qualitative research methods because they are well suited to exploration and discovery in an era of rapid and fundamental change. Qualitative researchers seek an understanding of *emergent reality*. To do so, they use methods of data collection and analysis that are flexible. Denzin and Lincoln

---

[2]Miles and Huberman (1994) are examples of this school of thought: "We think that social phenomena exist not only in the mind but also in the objective world and that some lawful and reasonably stable relationships are to be found among them" (p. 4).

(1994) describe this as "a *bricolage*, that is, a pieced-together, close-knit set of practices that provide solutions to a problem in a concrete situation" (p. 2).

Hackman (1985) explains further the value of qualitative research. First, he suggests that laboratory methods alone are not much help in producing practical theoretical knowledge about many challenges today because they ignore the significant, complex influence of the organizational context. Multiple methods and multiple data sources are needed to capture this complexity.

Second, he points out that field experiments do not produce practical theory because organizations do not hold still while we study them. Partnering with the organization and creating research that evolves with the organization is more likely to produce practical knowledge.

Third, Hackman suggests that searching for single causes of performance effectiveness makes it harder to learn about organizational conditions that foster good performance. In fact, system theory teaches us that many things may contribute to improved performance, some of which are additive, whereas others stand out as being among critical factors. The modus operandi developed by Scriven (1974), cited by Hackman, in which individuals generate lists of possible causes from multiple stakeholder perspectives, is one way to search out complex, overdetermined causation.

Fourth, Hackman questions the practical value of contingency models of behavior in organizations because they tend to exceed our ability to hold multiple contingencies in mind when making management decisions. How could we, for example, capture a moving picture of behavior that would allow us to see the way in which the choices people make at one point affect their future capabilities to act?

Finally, Hackman suggests that evaluation research often allows both researchers and managers to temporarily avoid the more important questions of organizational effectiveness. Research often counts productivity improvements without looking at the authority structure, the core technology and processes used, or the values and assumptions of management about human resources. Qualitative research would help to determine, instead, how to improve productivity through changes based on stakeholder perceptions, values, and practices.

Hackman shows us the value of qualitative, and mixed qualitative and quantitative, approaches to uncover the complex, multivariate nature of human organizations and performance. His assertions remind us that research can be a tool either to prove or to illuminate. Organizational researchers who are more fundamentally organizational interventionists are most likely to make a difference when they construct research in a manner that focuses on how organizations make meaning of events and phenomena rather than on the bare facts, devoid of context.

When Qualitative Research Is Most Appropriate

When, then, are qualitative approaches most appropriate in HRD? Qualitative research is useful (1) for building *new theory* rather than imposing existing frameworks on existing data and (2) for exploring uncharted territory (Marsick, 1990). Rowden (1995), for example, uses a qualitative multiple case study to explore the role of HRD in small to mid-size manufacturing companies that had long been overlooked in favor of large Fortune 500 companies. Hansen, Kahnweiler, and Wilensky (1994) use qualitative methods to collect and analyze stories that employees tell as they try to interpret their experiences. Researchers use these data to explore the yet-uncharted occupational culture of HRD.

Qualitative research also helps to understand a particular, situated phenomenon, such as the interpretations of a group of individuals around the meaning of quality or the factors to address when promoting organizational change. A focus on the specific context helps decision makers see potential traps to stated goals and determine more accurately what initiatives to take and when to introduce them. Swanson (1990) collected qualitative data from an educational enterprise to develop a model for planning, monitoring, and evaluating the process of implementing a new curriculum. The data, in turn, were used to improve the process for ensuring fidelity between intended curriculum and what is actually taught.

In another example, Elmes and Kasouf (1995) interviewed a cross-section of forty-four employees at four biotechnology firms in order to better understand what organizational learning looked like and what was interfering with the ability of biotechnology organizations to learn, given a stated need to do so for survival. Elmes and Kasouf found that the natural prediction of researchers for a scientific approach to organizational learning was competing with a market-induced push for results, no matter what the quality of the product. These insights were contextually based and illustrated by specific examples from the scientists and managers themselves. They further an understanding of organizational learning in general, and they also identify leverage points that need to be addressed if these biotechnology organizations want to increase organizational capacity to learn.

When combined with quantitative data, qualitative data can help to elaborate on the meaning of statistical findings. They also add depth and detail to findings. On the front end, qualitative methods are necessary when there is a lack of proven quantitative instruments or instruments need to be adapted to a particular situation. Qualitative methods are particularly appropriate when the research process needs to build buy-in from participants, such as in needs assessment or when forecasting future events or conditions. They may be more appropriate in formative evaluation studies and can strengthen summative evaluations by identifying unanticipated outcomes. In summary, many quantitative research studies in HRD can be strengthened by adding a qualitative component to the design.

Overview of the Qualitative Research Process

As noted earlier, qualitative researchers study things in their natural settings, attempting to make sense of, or interpret, phenomena in terms of the meanings people bring to them. The qualitative research methodology selected for a specific study should fit with the natural setting that is under investigation and be minimally intrusive. Thus, a high-quality qualitative inquiry method must be judged in terms of the fit with the selected natural setting, not simply against a pre-prescribed process as would more likely be found in quantitative research.

A logical place to start when thinking about the qualitative research process is to think of the general problem-solving method including the phases of defining the problem, listing all the alternatives, identifying the best alternative, implementing the alternative(s), and evaluating the process and results.

These are simple words that embrace complex phases of human endeavor that take place in complex natural settings. Therefore, a qualitative research study aimed at unearthing deeper meaning might deal with only one of the phases in a particular setting. It may be enough to pursue a study that only deals with the first phase of problem definition, for example, the issue of economic equity in the workplace. Even though the researcher may be personally shocked by the fact that top executives routinely make 300 times as much money as the lowest paid employee in their organizations, the researcher in this instance does not try to solve the larger perceived problem of equitably distributing the wealth generated by an organization to all contributors. Rather, a qualitative study focused on the meaning of equity in organizations and understanding the associated problems could be seen as the appropriate scope of an initial inquiry.

Patton (1990, pp. 40–41) approaches the issue of qualitative research design by identifying ten themes that are part of every qualitative inquiry strategy. Because of the situation-specific nature of qualitative inquiry, this approach is appropriate for judging the strengths of a qualitative study design. The ten themes are as follows:

1. *Naturalistic inquiry*—real world situations.
2. *Inductive analysis*—begins with collection of details that lead to generalizations.
3. *Holistic perspective*—phenomenon is understood as a complex system.
4. *Qualitative data*—detailed description is collected.
5. *Personal contact and insight*—researcher has personal contact with participants.
6. *Dynamic systems*—views object of study as dynamic and changing during the study.
7. *Unique case orientation*—each research case is unique and special.
8. *Context sensitivity*—places findings in a social, historical, and temporal context.
9. *Empathetic neutrality*—although the researcher cannot be completely objective, neither should the researcher use the process to advance personal agendas.
10. *Design flexibility*—the inquiry process is adaptive, potentially changing as the research process is conducted.

Qualitative Data Collection Methods

Qualitative researchers are required to collect and analyze data in order to describe routine and problematic moments and meanings in individuals and their organizational lives. Several general data collection methods are available:

- Interviews (individual and group)
- Questionnaires (open-ended)
- Observation
- Organization records

Qualitative researchers require first-hand information about organizations, processes, and the individuals involved. They must delve into the organization and its workplace issues to get accurate information. Each of the four methods has its appropriate uses, and each demands competence in searching for valid information.

Interviews (Individual and Group)

An in-depth interview method enables analysts to gather information from people in the workplace or people who connect in various ways to the organization and its processes: in person, in groups, and also by telephone. Such interviewing demands a high level of competence and commitment from the analyst. Interviews may be unstructured, such as informal conversation format, or structured, where a predetermined set of questions is used. Questions asked may be open-ended, such as when defining issues and themes, or more focused when researching specific issues.

Interviewing people in the workplace is a time-consuming but useful technique for discovering what happens at the organization, process, and/or individual levels. The skillful interviewer anticipates the need to establish a rapport with the interviewee or group of interviewees—not an easy task when questions of adequacy or efficiency of performance are involved. The interviewer is obliged to ask questions of people, using their language, to listen with respect, and to record accurate notes.

Interviewing is done with a critical eye to the process. The following checklist of questions will assist you in keeping your interviewing on track (Swanson, 1996):

___ Have I done my homework?

___ Am I talking to the best possible person, or would someone else be able to offer a more accurate account of the situation?

___ Am I getting straight information?

___ How do the responses of several people compare?

___ Is something being implied but left unspoken?

___ Am I perceived to be a confidante of management, or am I being trusted with knowledge of this situation?

___ Am I managing this limited interview time well?

___ What is the main message this person is giving me?

___ Is it important?

___ Have I discovered feelings and motivations as well as facts about this work situation?

___ Have I recorded many of the actual words of the respondent?

___ What is missing from the picture being painted here?

___ How do these interview data compare with data collected by questionnaire, by observation in the work setting, or by organizational records?

Interviews yield great quantities of information, which can be difficult to manage and analyze. Experienced interviewers know that you need to spend twice as long writing about the interview as you did conducting it.

Focus groups are a popular form of group interview. Krueger (1994, p. 16) defines focus groups in six parts: (1) people (2) assembled in a series of groups (3) possess certain characteristics and (4) provide data (5) of a qualitative nature (6) in a focused discussion. Thus, focus groups are different than other groups such as advisory groups or planning groups, which may have some but not all of these characteristics. The critical value of focus groups is that they enable the researcher to interview people more efficiently and that they capitalize on the group interaction around a topic. Focus groups are not appropriate in situations where the group interaction would inhibit discussion. For example, senior managers are often reluctant to discuss their units' weaknesses in front of other senior managers, who might use the information against them. Similarly, employees will usually not criticize their bosses when the boss is in the group. Thus, the design of the focus group is a critical consideration.

The following focus group moderating skills presented by Krueger (1994) capture the uniqueness of this technique: (1) mental preparation, (2) purposeful small talk and presentation strategy, (3) recording the group discussion, (4) the pause and the probe, (5) selecting the focus group location, and (6) being ready for the unexpected. It is beyond the scope of this chapter to discuss these in detail, but it is important to realize that the skills of the moderator in executing these steps are crucial to the research outcomes. Focus groups require a higher level of facilitation skill than interviews, which can bias the data collected if the researcher is not a strong facilitator. For example, a facilitator who does not design the focus group to control for power dynamics in the organization might not find any serious issues discussed and falsely conclude that issues do not exist.

Questionnaires (Open-Ended)

Deceptively simple, the open-ended survey questionnaire is often used as a prime qualitative data collection tool. Although often thought of as only a quantitative tool, surveys can also be used to collect qualitative data. For example, open-ended questions yield qualitative data that is analyzed the same as interview data. Good questionnaires of all types are difficult to develop, and getting sufficient numbers of responses from the target population is even more difficult. But done correctly, there is no tool more efficient for getting data from a large, dispersed population. Qualitative researchers often interview as a first step for discovering the most useful content for a questionnaire. The questionnaire also then offers a way to accurately evaluate the extent and the credibility of the facts and opinions gathered by interviews.

By keeping questionnaires as short as possible, you will ensure the good will of the respondents, and you will simplify the data analysis. Pilot-testing a questionnaire with a few respondents and if necessary rewriting questions can save you from gathering useless data.

Unless you are trained in content and/or statistical analysis, you would do well to acquire expert guidance in handling all phases of the questionnaire process. Too often the result of an inept questionnaire is garbled information that is useless to the analyst and ultimately to all the people who have spent their time and energy filling out the instrument.

The questionnaire process must begin with the questions: What do I want to know? and If I get it, how will I use this information? The process ends with, Did I discover what I wanted to know? and How can I use this information? These same questions are asked for every item on the questionnaire.

Assuming you have not let talk of data analysis discourage you from sending out a questionnaire, ask yourself the following: Did I receive a sufficient number of returned questionnaires? What did I find out? Are these data useful? Did I discover something that I should verify through a review of performance records or through observations or interviews? Do these data confirm or contradict what I have learned through other means?

Organization culture questionnaires, or culture surveys, are an important tool for human resource practitioners and scholars. They provide an effective and efficient method of gathering information from employees (Sleezer & Swanson, 1992).

Surveys must be organized around clear purposes and managed in a simple and effective manner (while maintaining the reliability and validity of the data). Employee perceptions are seen as a valid source of information as to the health of the organization! McLean (1988) has proposed thirteen culture categories, including organizational mission and goals, corporate management leadership, department management leadership, supervisory effectiveness, working conditions, productivity and accountability, communications, interpersonal and interdepartmental relationships, job satisfaction, employee compensation, employee career development, training and development, and training options. The critical features of such survey questionnaires are ensuring anonymity, the presence of an objective third party, and constructive feedback to the organization. Baseline data can be used to compare results to later surveys. The open-ended responses can be solicited and content analyzed and used for baseline comparisons.

Observation

Thinking, planning, imagining, and estimating are abstract human behaviors and, one would think, difficult to study. People express the results of their work performances through observable actions, however, and the qualities of their actions can be observed. When practiced systematically, observing people at work will yield a great deal of qualitative information about the work, the people, and the environment. Observing people at work requires considerable skill: great sensitivity and the ability to be unobtrusive are essential. To avoid altering the process or setting, the researcher must become part of the flow. The unobtrusive observer is more likely to perceive errors, problems, and creative solutions than is the intrusive observer.

Some activities happen more or less frequently than others, some take a longer or shorter time to complete, and some happen only at the beginning or the end of the month. Therefore, judging the length of required observation time can be difficult. One thing is certain: the longer you observe in a setting, the more you see. Before beginning to collect data, plan to observe long enough to be able to discriminate between events and behaviors.

Patton (1990) identifies five dimensions of observational designs that should be considered by qualitative researchers. Each of these dimensions, which are really continuous rather than discrete choices, affects the research process, analysis, and outcomes. Qualitative researchers have an obligation to carefully consider the impact of these choices on the data collected and interpretation of the results. The five dimensions are as follows:

1. *Role of the observer*—may range from a full participant in the process, observing as an insider, to an onlooker observing as an outsider.
2. *Portrayal of the observer role to others*—observers may make it known that they are observing (overt) or choose to remain anonymous to the group (covert).

3. *Portrayal of the purpose of the evaluation to others*—choices range from giving a full explanation of the purpose to everyone, to giving only partial explanations, to giving false explanations to hide the purpose of the evaluation so as not to change behavior.
4. *Duration of the observations*—observations may be one-time or long-term multiple observations.
5. *Focus of the observations*—observations may be made for one single or specific purpose (e.g., communication patterns in a group) or have a broad holistic focus (factors that affect group processes and effectiveness).

Be cautious when interpreting data derived from observation. Consider that your presence can change the situation and affect the data collected. Were you sufficiently prepared for the observation to understand what you were observing? How accurate are your data? Were you unable to record what you saw because of a lack of time or recording skill? Is that important? Does the observed behavior fall into phases or stages? Is it cyclical?

The popular truism that a picture is worth a thousand words applies equally to analysis work. The picture in the realm of most human resource development inquiry is the actual organization, the functioning processes, and the individuals working in them. First-hand observation provides a tier of information that cannot be obtained through the talk and paper of interviews and questionnaires.

Organization Records

Organizations keep records of many occurrences. These include strategic plans, brochures, absentee lists, grievances filed, units of performance per person, and costs of production. Policy manuals, procedure manuals, interoffice memos, minutes of board meetings, and the like are kept on file. Trends and cycles can often be spotted in these records. Clues to trouble spots or apparent contradictions to other data provide useful questions for follow-up. Ordinary, everyday organizational records are a great source of information for the alert researcher with skills in interpreting data.

Organizational records generally reflect the consequences of a problem situation, just as they may later reflect its resolution. Thus, organization records are most useful in zeroing in on the present state (versus a desired or future state). Caution must be taken in interpreting these data because they are generally collected for other purposes. How old are the data? How reliable were the collecting and recording methods? Be alert for aggregated information presented as averages that may hide major organizational issues.

Once you have verified the accuracy, considered the context of the organization records, and spotted any trends and problems, ask yourself if any of the data seem surprising, contradictory, optimistic, or problematic. The data should confirm or deny the facts gained from other data collection methods of interviews, questionnaires, and observations.

❖

Data Analysis Methods

Analysis of qualitative data takes place both during and after data collection. The critical skill in analyzing data *during* data collection is keeping the interpretation in line with the fact that there is only partial in-process data. Early overinterpretation of partial data is a serious threat to the validity of a qualitative study. Qualitative data can also be collected and analyzed within a single site and across sites. In large organizations, it is common for inquiry questions to transcend sites.

Because qualitative research data are primarily *words*, the best means of presenting the final data is through rich narrative. Yet, reports of this nature are often left unread. Executive summary reports that display matrices, charts, checklists, short text segments, and graphic metaphors help communicate to readers and entice them into the full text. Along the journey, the methods of making conclusions and information synthesis methods provide important assistance.

Making Conclusions

Twelve tactics for *generating meaning* among qualitative data have been proposed (Miles & Huberman, 1994). They are noted and described as follows:

1. *Counting*. A theme emerges from the data when something happens a number of times or in a consistent way.
2. *Noting Patterns*. Repeated themes, or causal explanations, that lead to theoretical constructs.
3. *Seeing Plausibility*. The common-sense explanation of data versus intellectual explanation.
4. *Clustering*. A tactical means of grouping fairly large ideas from the data into alternative conceptual bins.
5. *Making Metaphors*. A synthesis of the data into words that dramatize and/or characterize the meaning.
6. *Splitting Variables*. A pulling apart of the data as a means of keeping from totally integrated but invalid data interpretation.
7. *Subsuming Particulars into the General*. A conscious and deductive move to more general data categories (rather than intuitively clustering information).
8. *Factoring*. A logical sorting of large amounts of disparate data in the mind and in a manner analogous to statistical factor analysis.

9. *Noting Relations Between Variables.* Identification of the parts from the data and explanation of the connections between them.
10. *Finding Intervening Variables.* Identification of the unplanned-for variables and their impact on the context under investigation.
11. *Building a Logical Chain of Evidence.* The creation of a heuristic and/or algorithm to represent the data.
12. *Making Conceptual/Theoretical Coherence.* A grouping of discrete facts into lawful, comprehensible, and more abstract patterns.

Miles and Huberman (1994) go on to propose twelve tactics for *confirming the findings* from the data. These tactics confront the issue of validity. Because there are no core agreements about tests of validity in qualitative research, the following suggested tactics provide multiple avenues to the question of validity:

1. *Checking for Representativeness.* Is the finding representative? Vivid examples are not necessarily representative, and the researcher cannot assume there are many more to back them up.
2. *Checking for Researcher Effects.* What effect does the presence of the researcher have on the natural setting? The researcher affects the site and the site affects the researcher.
3. *Triangulating.* Do multiple sources of data agree? Independent measures of the same phenomena should agree.
4. *Weighing the Evidence.* Are the data of sufficient quality and quantity? All sources of data are not equal and should not be treated as equal.
5. *Making Contrasts/Comparisons.* Can the conclusion stand the test of contrast/comparison? The hard differences

approach must focus on important differences, not senseless variables.

6. *Checking the Meaning of Outliers.* Do the exceptions have an important story to tell? Paying attention to the outlier data could provide an excellent validation of the conclusions.

7. *Using Extreme Examples.* Do the extreme outliers tell us even more about the findings? Explaining extreme examples may be a way of getting at the core finding.

8. *Ruling Out Spurious Relations.* Do verified relationships mean causality? The related variables may in fact have an underlying casual variable that has not yet been identified.

9. *Replicating a Finding.* Does this phenomenon happen over and over? Findings that hold true in multiple sites are more credible.

10. *Checking Out Rival Explanations.* Have the rival explanations been seriously considered? Exploration of the rival explanations requires deeper consideration of the qualitative data.

11. *Looking for Negative Evidence.* What data exist that challenge the findings? Coming to a conclusion too early is the greatest threat to sound research.

12. *Getting Feedback from Informants.* What do those who gave you raw data think about your findings? This common-sense tactic also has cautions in terms of the delicacy of timing.

Data Synthesis Methods

Swanson (1996) informs us that experts describe eight synthesis techniques for dealing with large sets of ill-fitting data: reflection, two-axis matrix, three-axis matrix, flowchart, events network, dichotomy, argumentation, and graphic modeling.

Reflection. All of the eight synthesis methods involve reflective thinking. Analysts who use reflection as a synthesis tool have found their favorite places and times to think. Some walk, some stare out the window, some go to their special spots with a cup of coffee. Some think better in the morning, others at night. These reflective thinkers juggle their data until a pattern, an obvious truth, a powerful metaphor, a set of factors, or a detailed formula forms in their minds. When the researchers control the conditions under which they think, they gain control of the quality of their thinking.

Two-Axis Matrix. If analysts have a favorite method of synthesis, it is the two-axis matrix. The usefulness of this method is affirmed by the frequency with which it appears. In a two-axis matrix, one set of variables is displayed as a row of descriptive terms on the horizontal axis and the second set as a column of terms on the vertical axis. Where the two axes cross, cells common to two of the variables are formed. Individual cells may be filled with information, or they may be void. Either condition should hold some significance for the analyst. A void that should be filled is a clear signal that an important piece of data is missing.

One analyst we know uses the two-axis matrix to organize the content of each piece of research literature she has collected. She simply writes all the titles on one axis and classifies the items of information covered in all the pieces on the other axis. Then she checks off the cells by content and information source. The patterns of checks in the matrix cells provide a synthesis of the subject matter.

Three-Axis Matrix. To most of us, the three-axis matrix is not as familiar as the two-axis matrix. It is a cube shaped, three-dimensional object, unlike the flat two-axis matrix. The third axis is most often used to express a set of abstract variables such as judgments of quality, intervals of time, or types of things. Given the large quantity of individual cells produced by even the simplest of these models, it should be clear that the three-axis matrix is a powerful tool for breaking down and reconnecting a very complex subject. People who are not visually oriented may have difficulty in mentally slicing a three-axis matrix into its subcomponents.

Flowchart. Flowcharting provides a method for organizing and synthesizing information that contains input-process-output items, decision points, direction of flow, documentation or preparation steps, confluence and divergence, and extraction. Most human systems are process oriented. If the subject matter data contain inputs and outputs, careful study will reveal the elements of the process that fit between them.

Many data sets that do not initially appear to lend themselves easily to process-oriented thinking might benefit from such a synthesis. An analyst in a fast food chain store looked at the satisfied customers (outputs) and at the hungry customers (inputs). He used the metaphor of the flow of transactions from the hungry customer to the satisfied customer to synthesize the findings related to customer service.

Flowcharting is especially useful for mentally and visually walking through present and future organizational processes or for identifying blocks. Synthesis models of critical processes can lead to better understanding of system elements and policy relationships.

Events Network. Time-bound synthesis models that combine all the critical activities and events aimed toward the achievement of goals have proven their value to planners, managers, and consultants. Events networks are system oriented. They help take into account all the activity paths and events by which work toward an organizational goal is accomplished. Often such synthesis models are used to describe what should be rather than what is. More than a few subject matter analysts have used events networks to synthesize the masses of information needed for understanding and curing problematic systems.

Events networks can be made as complicated and precise as necessary. Some will require a huge expanse of fine print to show the lapses of time and the depth and breadth of activities undertaken to reach a goal. Some are computerized and help to calculate the total time and coordination efforts needed for large projects.

Dichotomy. One way to synthesize ambiguous subject matter is to fit the data into two mutually exclusive groups or camps, or contradictory issues. Chris Argyris (1993) used this synthesis method when he subsumed management practice into two categories, Espoused Theory and Theory in Use. He used the model to show managers the contradictions between what they said and what they did.

To work with diffuse subject matter, divide the data into two parts. Good or bad, yes or no, this or that type dichotomies help to clarify an unclear, undefined subject. Difficult or ambiguous subjects, such as older workers, become more clearly defined when they are synthesized with a dichotomy model.

Argumentation. Some research questions do not lend themselves to argumentation because of the irresolvable nature of the facts. Certain religious topics are a case in point. On the other hand, some seemingly irresolvable issues do lend themselves to reason and dialogue. Argumentation is a synthesis method aimed at resolving two or more theses, positions, or valuations of a subject matter. The question, Can I love my child too much? is probably not resolvable. Finding an answer to the question, What is the main societal condition that leads to sexual harassment? may be a resolvable issue.

Like the dichotomy, the argumentation method explores two opposing facets of an issue. Argumentation requires that you pose a best possible hypothesis and its supporting logic. You then disengage from this first hypothesis and propose a counter hypothesis with which to attack and test your first hypothesis. This intellectual attack provides the basis for modifying and refining the original hypothesis. The process ends with a resolution to the argument. Classical debate is a prime example of argumentation. The parties to a debate must attack their own arguments intellectually before those arguments are torn apart by their opponents during the debate.

Graphic Models. There is no limit when it comes to graphic models: organizational charts, product life-cycle diagrams, maps—these can be circular, spiral, triangular, tree-like. When analysts capture data in a particularly fitting graphic model, the data are easily more understood. Such models have an appealing, visual quality that stays with even the most casual viewer.

Linear graphic models are particularly useful for depicting the steps or phases or stages of a process. Simple linear models were used to organize and synthesize the subject matter of this book. The difference between a linear model and a multidimensional relationship model is important. Although the flowchart includes decision points, the linear model does not. In the linear model, no step is missed or skipped; all steps are experienced.

A graphic interaction model is appropriate when a synthesis model is needed to show the qualities, quantities, and directions of interaction among people or machines. The transactional nature of much of organizational life lends itself to the use of heavy and light, dotted or dashed arrows—whatever will help to synthesize the meaning of the transactions.

Conclusion

Qualitative research methodologies are increasingly being recognized as critical in helping answer the core questions facing the HRD profession. Many of the core questions facing the profession require a deep understanding of what is happening in real-life complex settings. The fact that HRD is a large field of practice and that it takes place in complex organizations suggests to the scholar that the very dynamic of being in the middle of the setting and a part of the process as it plays itself out is important.

Being comfortable with qualitative research methods requires researchers to begin the research process with a commitment to the journey. In addition, qualitative researchers should have an ability to gather large amounts of data, to learn from them, to adjust their thinking, and to synthesize the data for the purpose of deriving meaning.

References

Argyris, C. (1993). *Knowledge for action: A guide to overcoming barriers to organizational change*. San Francisco: Jossey-Bass.

Denzin, N. A., & Lincoln, Y. S. (1994). Introduction: Entering the field of qualitative research. In N. K. Denzin & Y. S. Lincoln (Eds.), *Handbook of qualitative research* (pp. 1–17). Thousand Oaks, CA: Sage.

Elmes, M. B., & Kasouf, C. J. (1995). Knowledge workers and organizational learning: Narratives from biotechnology. *Management Learning, 26*(4), 403–423.

Hackman, J. R. (1985). Doing research that makes a difference. In E. E. Lawler III, A. M. Mohrman, Jr., S. A. Mohrman, G. E. Ledford, Jr., T. G. Cummings, & Associates (Eds.), *Doing research that is useful for theory and practice* (pp. 126–149). San Francisco: Jossey-Bass.

Hansen, C. D., Kahnweiler, W. M., & Wilensky, A. S. (1994). Human resource development as an occupational culture through organizational stories. *Human Resource Development Quarterly, 5*(3), 253–268.

Krueger, R. A. (1994). *Focus groups: A practical guide for applied research* (2nd ed.). Thousand Oaks, CA: Sage.

Marsick, V. (1990). Altering the paradigm for theory building and research in human resource development. *Human Resource Development Quarterly, 1*(2), 5–34.

McLean, G. N. (1988). *Construction and analysis of organization climate surveys.* St. Paul: Training and Development Research Center, University of Minnesota.

Miles, M. B., & Huberman, A. M. (1994). *Qualitative data analysis* (2nd ed.). Thousand Oaks, CA: Sage.

Patton, M. Q. (1990). *Qualitative evaluation and research methods.* Thousand Oaks, CA: Sage.

Rowden, R. W. (1995). The role of human resource development in successful small to mid-sized manufacturing businesses: A comparative case study. *Human Resource Development Quarterly, 6*(4), 355–373.

Scriven, M. (1974). Maximizing the power of causal investigations: The modus operandi method. In W. J. Popham (Ed.), *Evaluation in education: Current applications.* Washington, DC: American Educational Research Association.

Sleezer, C. M., & Swanson, R. A. (1992). Culture surveys: A tool for improving organizational performance. *Management Decision, 30*(2), 22–29.

Swanson, B. L. (1990). *The development and evaluation of a model for planning, monitoring, and evaluating curriculum implementation.* Unpublished doctoral dissertation, University of Minnesota.

Swanson, R. A. (1996). *Analysis for improving performance: Tools for diagnosing organizations and documenting workplace expertise.* San Francisco: Berrett-Koehler.

Van Manen, M. (1990). *Researching lived experience: Human science for an action sensitive pedagogy.* Albany: State University of New York Press.

❖

Further Reading

Cohen, L., & Manion, L. (1985). *Research methods in education.* London: Croom Helm.

Flanagan, J. C. (1954). The critical incident technique. *Psychological Bulletin, 51*(4), 327–358.

Glaser, B., & Strauss, A. (1967). *The discovery of grounded theory.* Chicago: Aldine

Lewin, K. (1947). Frontiers in group dynamics. *Human Relations, 1*(2), 150–151.

Lincoln, Y. S., & Guba, E. G. (1985). *Naturalistic inquiry.* Thousand Oaks, CA: Sage.

Van Maanen, J. (1988). *Tales of the field: On writing ethnography.* Chicago: University of Chicago Press.

Watkins, K., & Brooks, A. (1994). A framework for using action technologies. In A. Brooks & K. Watkins (Eds.), *The emerging power of action inquiry technologies: New directions in adult and continuing education series* (pp. 99–111). San Francisco: Jossey-Bass.

Yin, R. K. (1984). *Case study research: Design and methods.* Thousand Oaks, CA: Sage.

C H A P T E R

Theory-Building
Research Methods

Richard J. Torraco
University of Nebraska

Few people other than theorists ever get excited about theories. Theories, like vegetables and televised golf tournaments, don't trigger provocative reactions from most people. Most theories, except those that are truly revolutionary, such as the contributions of Newton, Einstein, and Darwin, just do their jobs quietly behind the scenes. They may increase our understanding of a real-world event or behavior or they may help us predict what will happen in a given situation. But they do so without a lot of fanfare. However, like many other functions that we probably take for granted, theory has an underrecognized yet important role in the professional discipline of human resource development (HRD).

114

This chapter addresses the role of theory in HRD. The purpose of this chapter is to provide a straightforward discussion of what theory is and why it is important to HRD. In addition, we will discuss the methods we use to develop theories and the prominent theories that have influenced HRD practice.

What Is Theory and Why Is It Important?

For such an important tool, the basic features of a theory are quite straightforward. A theory simply explains what a phenomenon is and how it works. A theory explains the phenomenon by identifying its main ideas, or *concepts*, and by stating the relationships among these concepts. Concepts and their interrelationships are the elements of theory that are common to most methodologies for theory building.

We develop theories because, according to Dubin (1976), aspects of the real world are so complex that they need to be conceptually simplified in order to be understood. A well-constructed theory gives clarity to a complex phenomenon by providing a system for understanding its core ideas and interrelationships. For this reason, a simple, elegant theory that makes real-world phenomena comprehensible is preferable to a complex, elaborate theory.

Theory helps us out all the time. Our formal and informal theories regularly come to our assistance, whether helping us to solve everyday problems or providing explanations for complex situations we encounter in organizations.

A straightforward example illustrates the importance and pervasiveness of theory in our lives. We leave the house in the morning and go out to the car. It doesn't start. We instantly engage in a search for causes. We review possible culprits from recent experience that might be associated with the car not starting, in an effort to construct a "theory" of why it won't start. Although not consciously acknowledged, we know that a plausible theory can be tested, and if correct, the problem can be solved and we can be on our way. Our "theory" of why the car won't start can save the day.

Theory has shaped the most effective tools of our trade. The guidance afforded by theory is essential for reaching the highest levels of professional practice. Suppose there were no change theory to guide the management of organizational change. We would have no basis for anticipating and addressing the inevitable resistance to change encountered during significant organizational transitions. Imagine that there were no theories of work design to guide our efforts to organize work into processes and tasks for employees to perform. We would have no basis for apportioning work among employees in ways that promote job satisfaction and productivity. Theory is an invaluable tool for guiding practice and advancing the HRD profession.

❖

The Roles of Theory in HRD

The roles that theory serves in HRD are essentially the same as those served by theory in other disciplines. Indeed, theory's potential value for guiding scientific understanding, explanation, and prediction cuts across all professional disciplines. With the help of Campbell's synthesis of the roles of theory (1990), the following list of the most prominent roles served by theory is offered together with an example of each role in the context of human resource development.

Interpreting new research data. Theory provides a means by which new research data can be interpreted and coded for future use. Research is currently generating a great deal of data on the effects of transformed organizational structures (e.g., flatter designs, "downsized" organizations). Organizational behavior theory maintains that as the organizational structure changes, new relationships emerge among the individuals who function within the organization. Theory is warning us that we must pay more attention to changing employee roles as organizations take on new forms.

Responding to new problems. Theory provides a means for responding to new problems that have no previously identified solutions strategy. Technologically advanced work environments that remove workers further from concrete cues to performance increasingly contribute to worker anxiety and operational errors. Theories of work design and human motivation tell us that frequent feedback that is procedure-specific increases worker satisfaction and accuracy of performance. Knowledge from these theories can be applied to new work environments.

Defining applied problems. Theory provides a means for identifying and defining applied problems. Work performance problems are often defined in terms of training solutions. Yet theories of performance maintain that work performance has multiple determinants; knowledge and skill (the primary objects of training) interact with ability, motivation, and environmental factors (determinants upon which training has little or no effect) to produce the outcomes of performance.

Evaluating solutions. Theory provides a means for prescribing or evaluating solutions to applied problems. Organizational leaders often look to outside agents as the means for effecting change in their organizations. Yet organizational change theory suggests that the direction and commitment for change and criteria for its success must come primarily from within the organization itself.

Discerning priorities. Theory tells us that certain facts among the accumulated knowledge are important and others are not. Theories of learning and instruction suggest that the learning goal to be achieved is more important than the speed of achieving it; the match between the instructional method and the capability to be learned is more important than the choice of media; and the type of evaluation is often less important than assuring that some form of evaluation is used to demonstrate effectiveness.

Interpreting old data in new ways. Theory gives old data new interpretations and new meaning. Theories of motivation have recast the importance of extrinsic motivators for work, such as pay and perquisites. The use of money has had unintended consequences in cases where it has undermined the intrinsic rewards of work (pay displaces intrinsic fulfillment) and in cases where increasing the pay of one person (the CEO) has demotivated everyone else.

Identifying new research directions. Theory identifies important new issues and prescribes the most critical research questions that need to be answered to maximize understanding of the issue. An environment of increasingly scarce economic resources portends diminishing investments in human resource development. Yet human capital theory challenges the HRD profession to reframe this issue into one in which greater depth of human capital contributes to the renewal and expansion of human and economic resources.

In addition, theory provides members of a professional discipline with a common language and a frame of reference for defining boundaries of their profession. A profession's theory base prescribes both the knowledge domains and scope of practice over which a profession claims to have expertise. The depth of the theory base should be directly related to the scope of practice. Finally, a key role of theory is to guide and inform research so that it can, in turn, guide development efforts and improve professional practice. Thus, as a conceptual foundation for research and practice, theory serves a critical role in the advancement of the HRD profession. The vital role served by theory can be seen in the cyclical model shown in Figure 1.1 in Chapter One.

Planned Change: An Example of Theory Shaping Practice

We can see the main concepts of a theory and the important role it serves by examining a general theory of planned change and how it is applied in practice. A theory of planned change explains how planned change occurs in organizations and provides a straightforward example of how theory can be used to guide HRD efforts to initiate and manage organizational change.

A general theory of planned change emerges from prominent characteristics that are shared among three dominant theories of change. Lewin's work in *force field analysis* (1951), the *action research model* developed by French (1969) and Burke (1982), and Kotter's theory of *organizational transformation* (1996) are all theories of planned change that emphasize the need for establishing readiness for change, for diagnosing the problem or opportunity for which change is needed, and for planning and carrying out the change process. The main concepts of a general theory of planned change, synthesized from these theories, are presented in Figure 6.1.

Organizations faced with the need for change, whether stimulated by economic, technical, cultural, or other forces, often enlist the help of internal or external consultants to initiate and manage the change process. The general theory of planned change described in this chapter provides a stable basis for guiding the course of organizational change. HRD professionals have a central role in facilitating organizational change. Yet are change processes as typically carried out by organizations guided by sound theory? Do the main components of the theory (readiness, diagnosis, planning and implementation, and evaluation and institutionalization) guide the actions of HRD professionals in effecting change? Although each of the components of change theory serves an important role in guiding the change process, they are often not followed. A review of each stage of a typical change process, as it might occur with and without the guidance of theory, clearly reveals the importance of basing HRD practice on a solid theoretical foundation.

At the very outset of the change process, the *readiness* of the organization for change is either not assessed at all or assumed to

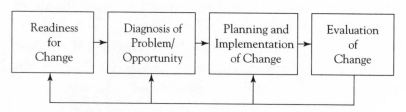

Figure 6.1. General Model of Planned Change

Source: Adapted from Lewin (1951), French (1969), Burke (1982), and Kotter (1996).

apply only to strategic and technical considerations. How would readiness be assessed if guided by theory? In addition to establishing the strategic need for organizational change, readiness would be assessed systematically to include human resource, technical, cultural, and structural readiness.

Executive management often conducts its own private, informal *diagnosis* of the organization. ("We need an increased market share within a lower cost structure. A consultant can help us with the internal transition to reach this.") When the data and recommendations offered by consultants are validated with the organization, such validation is usually done with management alone. The views of lower-level employees on organizational problems and opportunities are either not sought or are undervalued.

What does theory suggest should be the basis of organizational diagnosis? Rather than being limited to management's opinion or the consultant's views, theory-based diagnosis is the result of broader input from employees and is based on data, not opinion. A theory-based change approach solicits input to the change process from all who will be affected by it and responds to concerns about the proposed changes.

The *planning and implementation* of change generally follows a traditional business planning model. Given whatever organizational need has been identified at this point, responsibilities for change are assigned, goals are set, and measures and time frames are established. Common deviations from what is prescribed by change theory include not anticipating and addressing the inevitable resistance to change encountered during implementation and not empowering employees to act on a shared vision of where change will lead.

Evaluation is usually not included in long-term change processes. Consultants have long since separated from organizations by the time indications of the success or failure of change efforts first emerge. In addition, extended time frames for change and ongoing change in other related areas distort the relationship between a change intervention and outcomes. Theory underscores the need for feedback to management and employees about whether changes should be continued, modified, or suspended. In addition, progress against key organizational goals should be evaluated, even if success cannot be fully attributed to the change effort.

This review of the components of a general theory of planned change demonstrates the benefits of basing practice on theory. The theory of planned change brings an open systems perspective to the change process. It prescribes *readiness* and *diagnostic* activities that are broad based and inclusive, and it ensures that change *implementation*, such as work design or training interventions, is planned and carried out in ways that are consistent with the organization's social and technical systems.

The theory also demonstrates the long-term, iterative nature of change processes and suggests that organizations cannot be changed or "reengineered" once and for all. As is now evident after several years of experience with reengineering in organizations, many such efforts fail to achieve their purposes because they run afoul of established theories of how change occurs. Theory advises us that as organizational structures change and new employee roles and relationships emerge, we must pay more attention to the *whole system*—both the technical and human dynamics of work reorganization. Reengineering efforts not based in theory have produced a poor record of success, as reinforced by a recent observation by Michael Hammer, the management consultant who first developed *reengineering:* "[T]he number one source of [companies'] difficulties has been in this area of coping with the reactions of the people in the organization to the enormity of the change" (Hammer & Stanton, 1995, p. 119).

Change efforts, including reengineering, are but one example of how HRD practices are far more effective when they are informed by theory. Core theories, such as change theory, provide vital guidance for organizational change by offering an effective system for explaining and managing the change process. By clarifying our understanding of complex, real-world phenomena, theory can have a powerful influence on the effectiveness of HRD practice. But where do the basic concepts and interrelationships that comprise the theory come from in the first place? That is, how is a theory developed? The origin of theory and the methods researchers use to establish core theories of practice are examined next.

❖
Theory Building

Theory building is the process of modeling real-world phenomena. Researchers who develop theory (*theorists*) construct a model using the concepts and relational laws that, when fit together, best describe, explain, or predict the phenomenon they wish to model. Formal theory building is based on an understanding of what is known in areas closely related to the topic in which greater theoretical understanding is needed. For example, theorists have been developing models of the human performance system to better understand the factors associated with improvements in work performance. Theorists seeking to develop a model of the human performance system start with what is known in related areas upon which they can build a new theory. A theory can be based on what is already known in general systems theory (von Bertalanffy, 1950), human performance technology (Gilbert, 1978), and organizational performance systems (Kotter, 1978; Rummler & Brache, 1995). Each of these three domains is a kind of intellectual "bin" that contains ideas that contribute to the theory. Theorists continue to advance our understanding of human performance by building theories that more effectively explain ways in which human performance can be improved (Chi, Glaser, & Farr, 1988; Campbell, McCloy, Oppler, & Sager, 1993; Bereiter & Scardamalia, 1993). All researchers engaged in theory building, no matter how inductive their approach, should know which general concepts to include in a theory and the kinds of information contained in each conceptual bin. Researchers gain this insight from experience, from other related theories, and from the process of building conceptual frameworks for other kinds of research.

However, theory building, especially in the behavioral sciences, is not as disciplined and systematic a process as researchers would wish. There are no menus or lists of ideas for theorists to choose from, nor are there generic templates that can be modified to quickly produce a desired theory. Rather, theory building starts with an important problem from practice or with existing research in a related area upon which theorists carefully build new conceptual relationships. Weick (1989) likens theory building to navigating a ship by radar at night through a waterway filled with real and phantom objects. Like marine navigation at night, the theorist relies on representations of the environment in the form of existing concepts, new research findings, and intuition. Concepts are selected for the theorizing process based on how closely they model the real-world phenomenon they are supposed to represent. The criterion the marine captain uses to select navigation cues from the radar screen is the presence or absence of echoes that are treated as surrogates for real collisions. Similarly, the criterion for selecting concepts for theory building is the theorist's own judgments about the centrality of the concepts to the theory. Like the mariner's radar screen, these judgments are surrogates for real-world confirmation of events.

Theorists have only their own scholarly judgment to rely on during theory building. True confirmation of a theory's precision must await empirical research to test its value in the real world. Like the mariner's radar screen, the theorist has only indirect evidence of the accuracy of theory during theory building. Nevertheless, subsequent actions (piloting the ship and building the theory) unfold as if the evidence were direct. Both the mariner and theorist must make disciplined interpretations of available evidence, imperfect as it may be.

Methods of Theory Building

The literature available to guide theorists on methods of theory building is sparse and uneven. Traditional descriptions of theory building are focused on outcomes and provide little guidance on the processes theorists use to build theories (Freese, 1980). In addition, these approaches to theory building reflect the traditional philosophy of science and assume that the real-world phenomena to be modeled by theory are not influenced by the researcher's involvement and that the researcher can gain enough prior familiarity with the phenomenon to propose what its key concepts should be before theory building begins. This perspective on theory building reflects a philosophy of science called *positivism*. The theory-building works of Kaplan, Snow, Weick, and Dubin represent this approach and are reviewed in the next section.

In offering the notion of a scientific paradigm, Kuhn (1970) compelled philosophers and researchers to rethink the assumptions underlying the scientific method and paved the way for alternative, postpositivistic approaches to research in the behavioral sciences. *Naturalistic* approaches to research and theory building emphasize the importance of contextual influences on theory building and reflect the belief that the phenomenon being researched cannot be separated from the process of research. Naturalistic inquiry allows theory to emerge from data obtained from within an experience or practice setting.

One naturalistic approach is research conducted on a specific case or a limited number of cases, called *case study* research, which allows a more focused study and a richer description of the contextually bounded phenomenon. Researchers have used both positivistic and naturalistic approaches to developing theories from case studies. The positivistic approach to theory building through case studies is reviewed through the work of Yin and of Eisenhardt. Theory building using case studies from the naturalistic perspective is examined through the work of Robert Stake.

A second naturalistic approach, *grounded theory*, which allows theory to evolve during actual research through continuous interplay between analysis and data collection, is a prominent naturalistic approach to theory building. The grounded theory perspective is reviewed through the work of Strauss and Corbin.

Theory Building from a Positivistic Perspective

Kaplan (1964) discussed theory building as a vehicle for the advancement of knowledge in any discipline where knowledge growth occurs both *by intention* and *by extension*. Knowledge growth by intention occurs when a partial explanation of a whole domain is made more and more complete. Early theories explain key portions of the domain and, in doing so, highlight the need for subsequent theories. Knowledge growth in the domain is likened to gradually adding light to a dark room or bringing a microscopic field into sharper focus.

In the field of HRD, knowledge growth by intention is occurring in organization development (OD), which was once based almost exclusively on "normative-reeducative" change strategies and group process interventions. The demands of today's business environment require OD to further integrate its therapeutic intervention model and normative perspective with a realistic human resource investment perspective. The theory base of OD is expanding to provide a broader foundation for the strategic value of OD (Beer & Walton, 1990).

Knowledge growth by extension occurs when a relatively complete explanation of a particular domain is then carried over and applied to adjoining domains. A metaphor for theory building by extension is the creation of a mural scene by scene. The development and application of general systems theory to a wide range of professional disciplines illustrates this type of knowledge growth. Originally developed by the German biologist von Bertalanffy (1950), general systems theory was then applied to the fields of economics (Boulding, 1956) and mathematics (Rapoport, 1956), later to the study of organizations (Katz & Kahn, 1966) and human performance technology (Gilbert, 1978), and recently to the field of HRD (Jacobs, 1989).

Snow (1973) offered a three-phase, process model for theory building. Patterned after an early model for describing the operation of human memory, Snow's model is composed of (1) recognizing *metaphors*, (2) constructing *models*, and (3) organizing *metatheories*. The initial, loose conceptions of the theorist (metaphors) are further developed into formal representations (models) that are presented in graphic-pictorial, geometric, or symbolic-mathematical form. A metatheory develops as one or more successful models in the same area become widely confirmed and accepted as accurate descriptions of important phenomena. Using his three-phase model to build a theory of teaching, Snow identified the Bayesian sheep dog as a *metaphor* for the teacher's role in guiding the direction and development of a "flock" of students. The metaphor was further developed into an analytical *model* of key teacher-student interactions while maintaining the image of teacher as shepherd. Snow suggested that this evolving theory of teaching might become incorporated into a grander *metatheory* of teaching through integration with existing theories of behaviorism, instructional design, and human problem solving.

Snow defined metatheories as families or categories of theories that arise when an original theory stimulates further research leading to descendent and derivative theories that apply to the same domain. Metatheories become foundational structures upon which individual related theories can be built. Metatheories of interest to HRD that have given rise to related theories include learning theory, psychoanalytic theory, human capital theory, and general systems theory.

Weick (1989) argued that the inadequacy of theories in organizational studies has resulted from the inability of theorists to accurately represent the process of theorizing. He characterizes theory building as disciplined imagination, "where the 'discipline' in theorizing comes from the consistent application of selection criteria to trial-and-error thinking and the 'imagination' in theorizing comes from deliberate diversity introduced into the problem statement, thought trials, and selection criteria that comprise that thinking" (p. 516). Theories of higher quality are produced when theorists pay particular attention to three aspects of theory building: 1) accurate statements of the problem to be addressed by the theory are specified, 2) many diverse conjectures about how to solve the problem are offered, and 3) a large number of diverse criteria for selecting among these conjectures are applied. By elaborating on what the theorist actually does in working through the problem statement, thought trials, and selection criteria needed for theory building, Weick adds clarity and structure to the nebulous process of theory building.

More so than any of the theory-building strategies discussed so far, Dubin's (1978) eight-phase methodology for theory building lays out an explicit road map for the theorist to follow. The methodology offered by Dubin, a well-known writer on theory and theory building, is frequently used as a template for building theories in the behavioral sciences. The eight phases of theory building are as follows:

1. *Units* (i.e., concepts) of the theory
2. *Laws of interaction* (among the concepts)
3. *Boundaries* of the theory (the boundaries within which the theory is expected to apply)
4. *System states* of the theory (conditions under which the theory is operative)
5. *Propositions* of the theory (logical deductions about the theory in operation)
6. *Empirical indicators* (empirical measures used to make the propositions testable)
7. *Hypotheses* (statements about the predicted values and relationships among the units)
8. *Research* (the empirical test of the predicted values and relationships)

The first five phases of the methodology represent the theory-building component of Dubin's model, and the last three phases represent the process of taking the theory into real-world contexts to conduct empirical research. Although theorists must consider the entire scope of Dubin's model for effective theory building, theory building and empirical research are often separated, and each is conducted as a distinct research effort.

Case Study Research and Theory Building

A more recent approach to theory building is the use of case study research to develop theories. A case study, whether it is focused on a work team, an organization, or an entire community, is an instance drawn from a class. Case studies, more than other methods of study, allow researchers to focus specifically on a phenomenon of interest, and they offer the greatest potential for revealing the richness, holism, and complexity of naturally occurring events. This section shows the distinctly different perspectives of three authors, each of whom addresses the use of case study research for theory building—Yin, Stake, and Eisenhardt.

Robert Yin (1994) has developed a case study research methodology that he argues convincingly is a bona fide research strategy. Yin's case study research methods reflect the *positivistic* philosophy of science and are preferred, according to Yin, when "how" and "why" questions are being posed, when the investigator has little control over events, and when the boundaries between phenomenon and context are not clearly evident. Yin specifies two roles for theory in his case study research methodology.

First, unlike traditional ways of generalizing research results from sample to population, Yin uses theory to guide what he terms the *analytic generalization* of case study results. This occurs when previously developed theory is used as a template with which to compare the results of the case study. According to Yin, "when two or more cases are shown to support the same theory, replication may be claimed. The empirical results may be considered yet more potent if two or more cases support the same theory but do not support an equally plausible, *rival* theory" (italics in original) (p. 31). This is the basis for Yin's replication logic, which is essential to multiple case analysis.

The second, and more traditional, role for theory is as a conceptual guide for case study researchers to what is being studied. Theory development is part of the initial design phase of case study research, whether the purpose of research is the development or testing of theory. Theory provides a blueprint for conducting case study research, even if theory building is the primary purpose of research. Yin's case study methods allow theorists to elaborate upon and refine their initial theories.

Stake (1994) views case study research from a qualitative perspective and maintains that a case study is both the process of learning about the case and the product of our learning. Although Stake's own work on case studies strongly reflects his naturalistic interests, he suggests that researchers have different purposes for studying cases and identifies three distinct types of case studies to meet these purposes. It is significant that theory can be developed or refined through any of the three types of cases identified by Stake. The *intrinsic case study* is undertaken because the researcher wants a better understanding of a particular case. The purpose of study is not to explore an abstract concept or generic phenomenon, such as adult literacy or organizational restructuring. Nor is study undertaken because the case represents other cases or because it illustrates a particular trait, problem, or pattern. It is undertaken, quite simply, because of intrinsic interest in the case itself. The *instrumental case study*, on the other hand, is undertaken to provide insight into a particular issue or phenomenon. The case is of secondary interest and facilitates our understanding of something else. Although the case is examined in depth and its features are often documented in detail, this occurs to advance a better understanding of the external phenomenon. Instrumental interest extended to several cases is called a *collective case study*. The cases are chosen because the researcher believes that examining them will lead to better understanding or better theorizing about a larger collection of cases. As stated, each of these three types of case studies—*intrinsic, instrumental,* or *collective*—can effectively support the process of theory building.

Eisenhardt (1989) integrates positivistic and naturalistic perspectives on the use of case studies for theory building and, in doing so, serves as a middle ground between Yin's positivistic approach and the naturalistic view of case studies held by Stake. Eisenhardt acknowledges the distinctive value of the two approaches and combines them into a multistage process of building theory from case study research. Theorists using case studies work through the process of theorizing by (1) defining the research question, (2) selecting cases based on theoretical, not statistical grounds, (3) developing instruments and protocols for data collection, (4) entering the field to collect data, (5) analyzing data using within-case and/or cross-case analysis, (6) specifying hypotheses, (7) enfolding literature, and (8) reaching closure. Eisenhardt suggests that theory developed from case studies is particularly well suited to new research areas or research areas for which existing theory seems inadequate. In addition, it offers important strengths that arise from the intimate link with empirical evidence, such as novelty, empirical validity, and testability.

❖

Grounded Theory

Grounded theory is a general methodology for building theory that is grounded in data systematically gathered and analyzed. Theory evolves during actual research through continuous interplay between analysis and data collection. Data collection, analysis, and theory have a reciprocal relationship with each other. Rather than propose a theory to be proven, the researcher begins with an area of study and what is relevant to that area is allowed to emerge (Strauss & Corbin, 1990). A central feature of the analytic technique used in grounded theory is "a general method of [constant] comparative analysis" between theory and data (Glaser & Strauss, 1967, p. viii). Using this methodology, theory may be generated initially from the data, or existing grounded theories may be elaborated or modified as new data become available. Given an initial research question, interview data are collected from field settings, and one of several systems for coding and analyzing the data is selected by the researcher. Throughout the research process, theory is provisionally verified through a rigorous process of continuous matching of theory against data.

The theory that emerges is not seen as the discovery of some preexisting reality "out there." Theory is considered an interpretation and is therefore limited in both a temporal and contextual sense. Grounded theory can never be established forever, and its validity is eroded as contemporary social reality changes. These limitations notwithstanding, grounded theory can provide concise theoretical formulations for the complex phenomena encountered in organizations.

Core Theories Underlying HRD Practice

HRD has benefited from a rich foundation of theories, many having originated in related fields. Theories from other disciplines that have contributed significantly to the HRD theory base include general systems theory, human capital theory, theories of organization behavior, change theories, social learning theory, situated learning theory, and theories of leadership, job design, work motivation, human performance, and professional ethics. New and evolving theories from disciplines such as management, economics, education, psychology, and other fields closely related to HRD will continue to broaden the conceptual base that informs research and practice in HRD.

Although it is relatively young as a field of study, HRD has made progress in developing its own theories to explain phenomenon of prime interest to the field.

Using general systems theory as a foundation, Jacobs (1989) proposed systems theory as a unifying theory for HRD and developed a *human performance system* to show the systemwide impact of HRD. Marsick and Watkins (1993) developed a framework for promoting a "learning organization" based on the theoretical foundations of both reflective learning and action science. Swanson (1994) has promoted the perspective of "expertise for the purpose of improving performance" based on economic, psychological, and systems theories. Brooks (1994) developed a research-based framework showing how patterns of organizational learning are related to the distribution of power. Torraco (1994) observed that although jobs, work processes, and organizations are undergoing rapid change, methods for analyzing these entities have remained static; he developed a theory of work analysis to support more fluid analytical methods for changing work environments. Holton (1996) reconceptualized the four levels of evaluation based on the lack of theoretical or research-based linkages between satisfaction and learning or performance. These and other HRD researchers continue to develop and improve theories that are vitally needed to guide the work of all HRD professionals.

Conclusion

This chapter has addressed theory and theory building in HRD. It has provided a straightforward discussion of what theory is and why it is important to HRD. It has also described and illustrated the nature of theory building and methods used to develop theories. Most important, this chapter has emphasized that theory is an invaluable tool for guiding research and practice and for advancing the HRD profession as a whole.

References

Beer, M., & Walton, E. (1990, February). Developing the competitive organization: Interventions and strategies. *American Psychologist*, pp. 154–161.

Bereiter, C., & Scardamalia, M. (1993). *Surpassing ourselves: An inquiry into the nature and implications of expertise*. Chicago: Open Court.

Boulding, K. E. (1956). General systems theory: The skeleton of science. *General systems yearbook*. Ann Arbor: University of Michigan.

Brooks, A. K. (1994). Power and the production of knowledge: Collective team learning in work organizations. *Human Resource Development Quarterly, 5*(3), 213–236.

Burke, W. W. (1982). *Organization development: A normative view*. Reading, MA: Addison-Wesley.

Campbell, J. P. (1990). The role of theory in industrial and organizational psychology. In M. D. Dunnette & L. M. Hough (Eds.), *Handbook of industrial and organizational psychology: Vol. 1* (pp. 39–73). Palo Alto, CA: Consulting Psychologists Press.

Campbell, J. P., McCloy, R. A., Oppler, S. H., & Sager, C. E. (1993). A theory of performance. In N. Schmitt, W. C. Borman, and Associates (Eds.), *Personnel selection in organizations*. San Francisco: Jossey-Bass.

Chi, M.T.H., Glaser, R., & Farr, M. J. (1988). *The nature of expertise*. Hillsdale, NJ: Lawrence Erlbaum.

Dubin, R. (1976). Theory building in applied areas. In M. D. Dunnette (Ed.), *Handbook of industrial and organizational psychology* (pp. 17–39). New York: Wiley.

Dubin, R. (1978). *Theory building* (2nd ed.). New York: Free Press.

Eisenhardt, K. M. (1989). Building theories from case study research. *Academy of Management Review, 14*(4), 532–550.

Freese, L. (1980). Formal theorizing. *Annual Review of Sociology, 6*, 187–212.

French, W. (1969). Organization development: Objectives, assumptions, and strategies. *California Management Review, 12*(2), 23–34.

Gilbert, T. F. (1978). *Human competence: Engineering worthy performance*. New York: McGraw-Hill.

Glaser, B., & Strauss, A. (1967). *The discovery of grounded theory: Strategies for qualitative research*. Chicago: Aldine.

Gradous, D. B. (Ed.). (1989). *Systems theory applied to human resource development*. Alexandria, VA: American Society for Training and Development.

Hammer, M., & Stanton, S. A. (1995). *The reengineering revolution: A handbook*. New York: HarperCollins.

Herzberg, F. (1966). *Work and the nature of man*. Cleveland: World Publishing.

Holton, E. F. (1996). The flawed four-level evaluation model. *Human Resource Development Quarterly, 7*(1), 5–22.

Jacobs, R. L. (1989). Systems theory applied to human resource development. In D. B. Gradous (Ed.), *Systems theory applied to human resource development* (pp. 27–60). Alexandria, VA: ASTD Press.

Jacobs, R. L. (1990). Human resource development as an interdisciplinary body of knowledge. *Human Resource Development Quarterly, 1*(1), 65–71.

Kaplan, A. (1964). *The conduct of inquiry: Methodology for behavior science*. San Francisco: Chandler.

Katz, D., & Kahn, R. L. (1966). *The social psychology of organizations*. New York: Wiley.

Kotter, J. P. (1978). *Organizational dynamics: Diagnosis and intervention*. Reading, MA: Addison-Wesley.

Kotter, J. P. (1996). *Leading change*. Boston: Harvard Business School Press.

Kuhn, T. S. (1970). *The structure of scientific revolutions* (2nd ed.). Chicago: University of Chicago Press.

Lawler, E. E., & Associates. (1985). *Doing research that is useful for theory and practice*. San Francisco: Jossey-Bass.

LeCompte, M. D., & Preissle, J. (1993). The role of theory in the research process. *Ethnography and qualitative design in educational research* (2nd ed., pp. 116–157). San Diego: Academic Press.

Lewin, K. (1951). *Field theory in social science*. New York: HarperCollins.

Lincoln, Y. S., & Guba, E. G. (1985). *Naturalistic inquiry*. Thousand Oaks, CA: Sage.

Marsick, V. J., & Watkins, K. (1993). *Sculpting the learning organization: Lessons in the art and science of systemic change*. San Francisco: Jossey-Bass.

Patterson, C. K. (1986). *Theory of counseling and psychotherapy* (4th ed.). New York: HarperCollins.

Rapoport, A. (1956). The diffusion problem in mass behavior. *General systems yearbook*. Ann Arbor: University of Michigan.

Rummler, G. A., & Brache, A. P. (1995). *Improving performance: Managing the white space on the organization chart*. San Francisco: Jossey-Bass.

Snow, R. E. (1973). Theory construction for research on teaching. In R. Travers (Ed.), *Second handbook of research on teaching* (pp. 77–112). Chicago: Rand McNally.

Stake, R. E. (1994). Case studies. In N. K. Denzin & Y. S. Lincoln (Eds.), *Handbook of qualitative research*. Thousand Oaks, CA: Sage.

Strauss, A., & Corbin, J. (1990). *Basics of qualitative research: Grounded theory procedures and techniques*. Thousand Oaks, CA: Sage.

Swanson, R. A. (1994). *Analysis for improving performance: Tools for diagnosing organizations and documenting workplace expertise*. San Francisco: Berrett-Koehler.

Torraco, R. J. (1994). *A theory of work analysis*. St. Paul: Human Resource Development Research Center, University of Minnesota.

von Bertalanffy, L. (1950). An outline of general systems theory. *British Journal of Philosophical Science, 1*, 134–165.

Weick, K. E. (1989). Theory construction as disciplined imagination. *Academy of Management Review, 14*(4), 516–531.

Whetten, D. A. (1989). What constitutes a theoretical contribution? *Academy of Management Review, 14*(4), 490–495.

Yin, R. K. (1994). *Case study research: Design and methods*. Thousand Oaks, CA: Sage.

C H A P T E R

Case Study
Research Methods

Victoria J. Marsick
Columbia University

Karen E. Watkins
University of Georgia

The umbrella strategy of case study research is extremely useful
to human resource development (HRD). Case studies are one of
the most prevalent formats for conducting research and they are
often a combination of qualitative and quantitative inquiry. Yin
(1984), one of the best-known advocates of case study research,
defines this umbrella strategy as *"empirical inquiry that* investigates
a contemporary phenomenon within its real-life context; when
the boundaries between phenomenon and context are not clearly
evident; and in which multiple sources of evidence are used"
(p. 23) (Yin's italics).

Case studies may seek answers to a simple, short-term question—for example, in what ways the human resource (HR) roles

in a reengineered company have changed; or they may focus on complex, longer-term concerns, such as tracing the path of organizational learning. The unit of analysis may also vary: it may involve *one or more individuals*, as in a study of the emerging nature of the job of the chief learning officer; or a *bounded social unit*, as in a study of self-directed or virtual teams, customer-supplier chains, or action learning program groups; or a *much larger unit of analysis*, as in an analysis of relationships among those involved in a complex partnership program in which a company, unions, and community colleges in several states retrain technical employees.

Key to the way in which the study is designed is this rule: do the researchers seek to build theory or simply describe the unique experience of those in a given situation? This will influence the way in which the research question is posed, the sample selected, methods chosen, and data analyzed. Stake (1994) uses this rule to elaborate on three basic types of case study: (1) *intrinsic*, that is, unique to one particular situation; (2) *instrumental*, that is, used to understand an issue or refine theory; or (3) *collective*, that is, involving multiple cases in order to shed light on a complex phenomenon or population.

❖

Procedures

There is no one best procedure for conducting case study research. As Stake (1994) puts it, "Perhaps the simplest rule for method in qualitative case work is this: Place the best brains available into the thick of what is going on. The brain work ostensibly is observational, but more basically, reflective" (p. 242).

The case study researcher does typically follow the steps below but not necessarily in a linear, step-by-step fashion (Cohen & Manion, 1986; Merriam, 1988; Stake, 1994; Yin, 1984):

◆ Identifying a focus and assumptions
◆ Using the literature
◆ Bounding the case, that is, deciding on a unit of analysis and sample
◆ Selecting data collection methods that are appropriate to the task
◆ Analyzing data for patterns as they emerge
◆ Describing and interpreting the phenomenon in light of what is known

Identifying a Focus and Assumptions

Case study researchers do not begin their work with a blank slate, but their focus is more generally stated than the carefully constructed hypotheses of quantitative research because their study is essentially exploratory. For example, Marsick and colleagues embarked on a collaborative case study of team learning (Kasl, Marsick, & Dechant, in press). The focus of the study was to describe in people's own words what took place when teams learned and to identify what people perceived to be factors that facilitated or impeded that learning. As in all such studies, these researchers had to first identify, clarify, and subsequently refine presuppositions and hunches—their own and those held by others in the field. For example, because of their grounding in John Dewey's work, their cognitive filters led them to expect people to learn when they encountered problems through the interaction of action and reflection. But they did not start with a hypothesis. Their research question was broadly conceived—

in essence, Do teams learn, and if so, what does team learning look like?

Case study researchers also need to identify the lenses through which they will design the study and interpret the phenomenon. Denzin and Lincoln (1994) call these first steps in the research process understanding self as a multicultural subject and understanding one's own theoretical paradigms and perspectives.[1]

Using the Literature

Existing literature serves as a guide, but the case study researcher uses it differently than in hypothetical-deductive studies in which an exhaustive search of the literature is used to frame hypotheses against which data are collected. In qualitative case studies, literature does help to frame the initial focus of the study. We began our study of team learning, for example, with a broad reading of literature on individual and organizational learning and on group dynamics (Kasl, Marsick, & Dechant, in press). As data are analyzed and themes emerge, the case study researcher goes back to the literature for deeper understanding of the theme and clues to refine focus, questions, and methods. We found, for example, that the culture of the technical professional influenced the way in which data analysts understood the concept of team and thus the way in which they interpreted the division of work as they formed self-directed teams. We went back to the literature to better understand technical professionals.

The researcher goes back to the literature again and again. The literature then helps frame data analysis. In the final stages

---

[1]Guba and Lincoln (in Denzin & Lincoln, 1994, and elsewhere), for example, illustrate the way in which methods of inquiry vary given differences in beliefs in four inquiry paradigms (positivism, postpositivism, critical theory, and constructivism).

of writing up our team learning study, for example, we found ourselves returning continually to the literature on group dynamics
to understand how it relates to, and is differentiated from, team
learning.[2]

Bounding the Case

The case is bound by a focus either on unique description or on
theory refinement and building. The HR practitioners, for example, may primarily be interested in analyzing the dynamics of an
innovative executive development program or an experiment in
team compensation and reward systems. The situation dictates
the selection of the people to be interviewed and the situational
variables to be studied. If insights are to go beyond one unique situation, the sample must be both broad enough to describe a range
of differences and influences and deep enough to provide rich description that is not totally idiosyncratic. For example, Elmes and
Kasouf (1995) explain the way they bound their multiple case
study of organizational learning in biotechnology companies:

> Our purpose in interviewing employees at four companies (dif-
> ferent in size and developmental stage) in different roles (sci-
> entists, managers and technicians) and at different levels
> within their organization (senior management, middle man-
> agement and non-managerial), was to identify the similarities
> and differences in patterns of response within and across roles,
> levels and firms [p. 406].

---

[2]Some qualitative researchers advise holding off in one's reading of the literature
until very late in the stage of data analysis because analysis is inevitably influenced
by one's conceptualization of the area of study. Glaser and Strauss (1967), for
example, suggest that grounded theory begin with a broad reading of the literature
but that focus be held off until one has completed an initial phase of data collection
and analysis. Van Manen (1990) advises that in phenomenological studies, the
questions be very broad and that literature be analyzed only after data have been
summarized and checked with respondents to ensure that they reflect their lived
experience.

If the researcher wants to refine or build theory, he/she will need to sample for people and conditions that will richly illustrate the phenomenon as well as delimit it. Kasl, Marsick, and Dechant (in press), for example, did case studies in two companies under different conditions to identify and describe the dynamics of team learning from the team members' perspective. The first company, a petrochemical company, was moving to participative management. The researchers chose to talk to a diagonal slice of people at many different levels, with various functions, and who worked in many different teams. This enabled them to paint a broad picture of what it looked like to learn in teams under different conditions. In the second example, they dug deep into the nature of team learning in three groups in an entire department that was reorganizing as self-directed teams. Their doctoral students are now advancing the theory by seeking to delimit the model that they developed through case studies of team learning, looking in different types of organizations and with different kinds of professional groups.[3]

Selecting Data Collection Methods

Case study utilizes a wide variety of data collection methods. The researcher seeks many ways to build a picture of experience. Denzin and Lincoln (1994) suggest that "the researcher-as-*bricoleur* uses the tools of his or her methodological trade, deploying whatever strategies, methods, or empirical materials as are at hand (Becker, 1989). If new tools have to be invented, or

---

[3]Two dissertations have been completed at Teachers College, that of Stephen John (1995), who studied two teams in an international financial services organization, and Carol Gavan (1996), who studied two teams of nurses. Other studies in progress include two replication studies in corporate settings (Ed Oxford and Joyce Rogers); one in a health care setting (Patricia Shephard); and a study of conflict in relationship to team learning (Alfonso Sauquet).

pieced together, then the researcher will do this" (p. 2). Multiple data collection methods are often used to triangulate sources and strategies in order to corroborate findings and to offset the shortcomings of any given method (Denzin & Lincoln, 1994).

Rowden's (1995) comparative study of HRD in small to midsized manufacturing companies, for example, draws on three of the most frequently used methods in case study: interviews, onsite observation of a sample of activities, and document analysis. Hansen, Kahnweiler, and Wilensky (1994) also use interviews and observation, but they build their interviews around critical incidents in the form of narrative stories selected and told by subjects, as well as line drawings depicting typical work situations that subjects could select to support their storytelling. It is also common to include simple descriptive statistics, for example, a Likert scale questionnaire collecting subject ratings relevant to the topic or empirical baseline data that are regularly collected by the organization.

Analyzing Data

Case study researchers are comparable to detectives. Their focus guides their analysis. As they collect data, they analyze it through what is often called a constant comparative method (Glaser & Strauss, 1967; Lincoln & Guba, 1985). They continuously reflect on the meaning of what they hear and observe and the direction in which they should next go to shed light on their focus, constantly comparing the data against the themes and looking for data that both confirm or disconfirm their interpretation. Case study research begins with a broad scan of the environment and, through an iterative process of reflective analysis, increasingly narrows the focus to that which emerges from the voices of those in the study.

Although strategies for analysis vary with data collection procedures, case study researchers continually recognize that interpretation is just that! Member checks help to ensure that the data reported reflect the interviewees' viewpoints, but their views are also subject to selective memory and interpretation. Because of the limitations of retrospective recall, interviewees might well have reconstructed their views due to intervening perceptions and events, even if their original perceptions and memory are accurate. The act of interviewing is itself an intervention in that it causes people to consciously reflect on experience that otherwise might lie fallow. Also, of course, the interviewer brings his or her own cognitive and emotional filters to interpretation.

The degree to which qualitative case study researchers simply report on differences in interpretation versus attempt to reconcile them through analysis is reflective of the degree to which the researcher thinks there is a truly objective reality to be identified or simply multiple realities to be examined. All case study researchers nonetheless do strive to acknowledge and report subjective differences as they proceed and in relation to available objective data. They continually make their foci and hunches as explicit as possible. They check their interpretations with other researchers and the people they are studying. They seek data that disconfirm their hunches to keep open to other views. They frequently write up lists of assumptions as they work, typically keep a journal of some kind in which they identify beliefs and record hunches, raise questions to explore and corroborate by talking with other people and collecting additional data, and review what they do or do not know about the phenomenon under focus.

Describing and Interpreting the Phenomenon

It is a challenge to systematically and fully describe the richness of data in a case study without overwhelming the reader and, when appropriate, to use the case study to refine and build theory. Good case studies tell a story, but the viewpoint and purpose of the story can vary. Stake (1994) points out, "We cannot be sure that a case telling its own story will tell all or tell well, but the ethnographic ethos of *interpretive* study, seeking out emic meanings held by the people within the case, is strong" (pp. 239–240). Stake goes on to list at least seven presentation styles identified by John Van Maanen (1988): "realistic, impressionistic, confessional, critical, formal, literary, and jointly told" (p. 240).

Whatever the style, case studies frequently both report the details of the story in a somewhat journalistic fashion and then include commentary that interprets the story. When the study's focus is theoretical, the commentary often links findings to other interpretations and frameworks. Brooks (1994), for example, illustrates a classic reporting format in her study of power dynamics vis-à-vis team learning. She first tells the unique story of groups that she has called the empowered team, the "A" team, the lost team, and the people's team. The reader learns the experience of each team from its own perspective. Brooks then uses the details presented in each story to discuss four research questions and to generate propositions grounded in these data regarding the nature of team learning, the impact of power differences on team learning, the impact of organizational structures and policies on team learning, and historical and cultural patterns in relationship to team learning. She concludes by examining the nature of power in the literature and using this richer conceptual understanding to suggest the ways in which power dynamics function to foster or impede team learning.

Case studies are frequently criticized for their potential lack of rigor, limited generalizability, and difficulty in reporting findings that can be overwhelming in rich description. Yin (1984) suggests that none of these criticisms is true solely of case study research. As he explains, rigor can be lacking in experiments and surveys as well, though the criteria for determining rigor in case studies are not standardized, as they are for quantitative experimental studies. However, as Lincoln and Guba (1985) point out, the criteria for rigor differ in qualitative research because its purpose differs.[4] Case studies are often used to describe or explain phenomena and to generate theory, not just test it—which can also hold for some experiments and quantitative studies. Thus, with some exceptions—typically multicase research using both qualitative and quantitative data—case studies are not meant by themselves to be generalized. However, rich quantitative and descriptive data across cases enable readers and researchers to compare case findings and ultimately build generalizable theory.

Finally, the case study reports a larger volume of description and must present enough of it to provide an audit trail, while at the same time being sufficiently selective so that the reader can see the forest and not just the trees. Case studies are not meant to produce crisp, focused rules of thumb; on the other hand, the stories they contain often speak more meaningfully to readers than do hypotheses stripped of context.

Action Research: A Case Study Methodology Defined and Illustrated

One common problem-solving strategy in organization development is that of action research. Fundamentally, most organization development approaches consist of a cycling among diagnosis, intervention, evaluation, or reflection on the results, followed by new action or intervention. This cycling between

[4]Lincoln and Guba (1985) propose the following four criteria for establishing trustworthiness in the naturalistic paradigm, as alternatives to the conventional criteria of internal validity, external validity, reliability, and objectivity: credibility, transferability, dependability, and confirmability.

researching a problem situation and trying out action experiments to solve the problem is known as *action research* and can be a form of case study research if followed with rigor. Action research is a problem-solving method first developed by Kurt Lewin, who coined the term in about 1944 (Kemmis, in Kemmis & McTaggart, 1988).

Several streams of action research have emerged. Chein, Cook, and Harding (1948) suggest four types:

1. *Diagnostic,* in which the researcher/scientist diagnoses a problem and makes recommendations for change
2. *Participant,* in which the actors learn to take action and to conduct research, now called *participatory action research* (Whyte, 1991)
3. *Empirical,* in which the actors document action for research and reflection
4. *Experimental,* in which there is controlled research on different action alternatives

Argyris and Schön (1991) define action research as follows:

> Action research takes its cues—its questions, puzzles, and problems—from the perceptions of practitioners within particular, local practice contexts. It bounds episodes of research according to the boundaries of the local context. It builds descriptions and theories within the practice context itself, and tests them through *intervention experiments*—that is, through experiments that bear the double burden of testing hypotheses and effecting some (putatively) desirable change in the situation [p. 86].

Contribution to knowledge is in the area of research on intervention. Participants must learn a mode of reflection (the action research technology) and participate in solving self-diagnosed problems. Kemmis and McTaggart (1982) define action research as

> a form of collective self-reflective enquiry undertaken by participants in social situations in order to improve the rationality and justice of their own social or educational practices, as well as their understanding of these practices and the situations in which these practices are carried out [p. 5].

Self-understanding and transformation is the goal in this research. Contributions to knowledge are likely to be in the area of reflective learning and strategies to improve the rationality and justice of educational practice. The emphases in each of these definitions are quite different.

Peters and Robinson (1984) examined the works of eleven action researchers and identified twelve general characteristics and three idiosyncratic characteristics. Those characteristics appearing most often were that the research was problem focused (11), collaboratively conducted and participatory (11), action oriented (11), an organic or cyclical process (8), and scientific (8). Other categories mentioned less often involved terms that often overlapped in meaning: normative, ethically based, experimental, reeducative, emancipatory, stress on group dynamics, and naturalistic. Using Peters and Robinson's classification, it is clear that the research emphasis implied by the categories *scientific* and *experimental* has less priority among many of these practitioners of action research than does the action orientation or problem-solving focus.

We conclude that action research uses the tools of scientific research in order to collaboratively solve problems in organizational and practice contexts. In part because it is responsive to its context and directed at change, action research is likely to take many forms and is equally likely to be normative or value laden.

Chein, Cook, and Harding (1948) state that action researchers are required to not only make discoveries but also to see that these discoveries are applied. In other words, the research is valid if it is applied in a particular context and works to solve the original presenting problem. The answer in the laboratory is not an answer in action research until it works in context. Argyris and Schön (1991) add that it is the quality of the inquiry process and the interpersonal skill of the action researcher that determine the validity of their accounts. For example, critiquing the action research project conducted by Lazes at Xerox Corporation, Argyris and Schön note that appropriate rigor also involves a critical test of the claims of the researcher. Perhaps the interventions work because other conditions in the context (e.g., financial exigency) force them to and hence they are not likely to work again in other contexts. Argyris and Schön call for an operational description of what the researcher actually did and critical reflection on the claims or attributions he or she makes about the achievements of the process. In this way, the research can be replicated and competing explanations (the negative case example) may be examined for the research results. They suggest that from the action researcher's perspective, "the challenge is to define and meet standards of appropriate rigor without sacrificing relevance" (p. 85).

Participants in action research programs expect to be treated not as objects or even subjects but as co-researchers engaged in "empowering participation" and in "co-generative dialogue" between "insiders and outsiders" (Elden & Levin, 1991). In action research, truth is in the process of inquiry itself. Was it reflexive and dialectical? Was it ethical and collaborative? Did participants learn new research skills, attain greater self-understanding, or

achieve greater self-determination? Did it solve significant practice problems or did it contribute to our knowledge about what
will *not* solve these problems? Were problems solved in a manner that enhanced the overall learning capacity of the individuals or system? These are the types of questions that must guide
action research.

A project conducted at a Southwestern high technology company illustrates these points. Action researchers met with a group
of individuals nominated by the organization and trained them
in action research and in the critical incident technique for data
collection. Members met with a group process facilitator and decided to focus on issues of empowerment in the organization.
Team members conducted critical incident interviews in their departments, asking for an illustration of a time when individuals
felt empowered and another when they felt disempowered.
Themes were identified once all of the incidents had been written up, pooled into one transcript, and looked at as a whole by all
team members. Team members asked to present their findings to
senior management. Because a significant portion of the data suggested that what most disempowered members of the organization
was a "culture of public humiliation" produced by managers' interactions with their subordinates, the response of management
was predictable.

Senior managers' responses focused on the way in which individuals had focused on personal rewards over team rewards and
on blaming managers rather than on taking personal responsibility. On the other hand, the organization had seen a similar
pattern in climate surveys and had already decided to launch a
major management training initiative focused on helping managers move toward a model of leadership more consistent with
coaching than reward and punishment. The impetus for the
management training program came from a level above the

senior managers who received the action research report. This project illustrates the way in which action research contributes strongly to deeper diagnosis and problem solving. Although the research was strong, the change implications and planning for change responses were less effective. Participants prepared at length to present the data and to handle what they anticipated would be defensive responses but did not couch their recommendations in terms of a viable change plan.

Further action in this context might have looked at what encouraged this culture of public humiliation. For example, one team member described how his manager came to a meeting of his supervisors carrying a big brown paper bag with two holes cut out of it. He placed the bag over the head of one supervisor and announced, "I would wear a bag over my head too if my production numbers were as poor as yours are." This example suggests that one potential reason for the culture of public humiliation is the pressure on managers to increase production quotas. Or the action researchers might have studied the effectiveness of the management training program in addressing the culture. We would predict that it would be highly likely to be ineffective if managerial rewards continue to focus on productivity quotas. Ideally, through recurring cycles of research, we would identify a root cause and then try to identify the issue. Inquiry would then focus on determining whether the experiment undertaken really addressed the root cause.

Action research is characterized most by its focus on producing change in the organization. Data collection methods used may be either qualitative or quantitative and can even include experimental methodology. But the goal is to determine what change is needed, what works, what action experiments to try and how they turn out, and how fundamentally to address the presenting organizational problem. Kurt Lewin (1947) himself explains its power:

The research needed for social practice can best be characterized as research for social management or social engineering.
It is a type of action-research, a comparative search on the
conditions and effects of various forms of social action, and research leading to social action. This by no means implies that
the research needed is in any respect less scientific or 'lower'
than what would be required for pure science in the field of
social events. I am inclined to hold the opposite to be true
[pp. 150–151].

Action research, like case study research, is highly dependent
on the skills of the researchers, the organizational context, and
the capacity to produce knowledge that is contextually valid.
Like all human change, this is indeed difficult. Action research
is primarily used in human resource development as a problem-
solving approach to quality improvement teams, to needs assessment, to benchmarking, and to cultural change. What would
enhance human resource developers' use of action research is a
more concerted effort to publish knowledge for larger audiences,
beyond the single organization case study, so that the learning
from each action research project might add to our repertoire of
knowledge about changing human systems (Watkins, in Watkins
& Brooks, 1994). Until we reach that point, action research will
continue to be more useful as an intervention process than as a
research method.

Guidelines for Contracting for
Case Study Research

Action research is not the only framework within which case
study research can be conducted. The *critical incident technique* is
another inquiry tool that is extremely useful when the goal is to
identify experiences that are especially meaningful because they

remain vivid in the minds of those experiencing them.[5] *Grounded theory studies* (Glaser & Strauss, 1967) are frequently used to build theory over many studies, as Gersick (1989) has been doing in creating a new paradigm for group development that departs from the time-honored stage theory.

These and other strategies can assist the practitioner, but the questions to ask in designing case study research differ from pure theory, quantitative, or qualitative research. As we conclude, we offer some guidelines to assist in contracting for case study research.

1. Clarify the focus for the research, but do not draw the net too tightly. Tell everyone involved that you expect the research itself to clarify the focus as the research proceeds. The need for problem reframing is reason enough to conduct studies when it is not clear where to focus energy.

2. Take advantage of the flexible nature of case study research to involve key stakeholders in critical decisions as the study proceeds. The payoff is enhanced by using the data to educate stakeholders along the way and increase their likelihood of "owning" the data and subsequent solutions.

3. Select samples based on unique experience with the phenomenon to be examined, as well as situations where the negative case is highly likely, so that you can contrast the factors that are likely to influence both positively and negatively. Seek both breadth and depth in your sample. Decide how broadly you need to cast your net in depicting the phenomenon.

---

[5]Flanagan (1954) developed the Critical Incident Technique (CIT) as an outgrowth of research he was doing with the U.S. Army Air Force in World War II. The behavioral event interview technique (BEIT) uses critical incidents to develop competency models. A specialized use of critical incident study is the action science case (Argyris & Schön, 1991).

4. If you are contracting with outside researchers, ask for a research design, and in addition ask for past experience in changing the design as new findings emerged. Look for variety in the researcher's repertoire of data collection methods.

5. Where appropriate, collect descriptive statistics to verify the extent of key findings and to counteract claims that stories are only local reporting.

6. Ask for a plan to defend the trustworthiness of findings that is suited to case study research. As part of this plan, ask the researchers to clarify the assumptions and hunches they bring to the study, and ask them for their thinking about the audit trail that they will create.

7. Develop a plan for checking findings with what has been learned elsewhere through research on this phenomenon and for using these insights both to shape decisions during the research and to write up findings.

8. Decide on several formats for reporting findings to different stakeholders so that sufficient information is provided to ensure credibility without overwhelming readers in too rich a description.

❖

References

Argyris, C., & Schön, D. (1991). Participatory action research and action science compared. In W. F. Whyte (Ed.), *Participatory action research* (pp. 85–96). Thousand Oaks, CA: Sage.

Becker, H. S. (1989). Tricks of the trade. *Studies in Symbolic Interaction*, 10, 481–490.

Brooks, A. K. (1994). Power and the production of knowledge: Collective team learning in work organizations. *Human Resource Development Quarterly*, 5(3), 213–235.

Chein, I., Cook, S., & Harding, J. (1948). The field of action research. *American Psychologist*, 3, 43–50.

Cohen, L., & Manion, L. (1986). *Research methods in education*. London: Croom Helm.

Denzin, N. A., & Lincoln, Y. S. (1994). Introduction: Entering the field of qualitative research. In N. K. Denzin and Y. S. Lincoln (Eds.), *Handbook of qualitative research* (pp. 1–17). Thousand Oaks, CA: Sage.

Elden, M., & Levin, M. (1991). Co-generative learning: Bringing participation into action research. In W. F. Whyte (Ed.), *Participative action research* (pp. 127–142). Thousand Oaks, CA: Sage.

Elmes, M. B., & Kasouf, C. J. (1995). Knowledge workers and organizational learning: Narratives from biotechnology. *Management Learning, 26*(4), 403–423.

Flanagan, J. C. (1954). The critical incident technique. *Psychological Bulletin, 51*(4), 327–358.

Gavan, C. (1996). *Team learning within nurse teams in a home care organization*. Unpublished doctoral dissertation, Teachers College, Columbia University, New York.

Gersick, C. J. (1989). Marking time: Predictable transitions in task groups. *Academy of Management Journal, 32*(2), 274–309.

Glaser, B., & Strauss, A. (1967). *The discovery of grounded theory*. Hawthorne, NY: Aldine.

Guba, E. G., & Lincoln, Y. S. (1994). Competing paradigms in qualitative research. In N. K. Denzin & Y. S. Lincoln (Eds.), *Handbook of qualitative research* (pp. 105–117). Thousand Oaks, CA: Sage.

Hansen, C. D., Kahnweiler, W. M., & Wilensky, A. S. (1994). Human resource development as an occupational culture through organizational stories. *Human Resource Development Quarterly, 5*(3), 253–268.

John, S. (1995). *A study of team learning in a professional services company*. Unpublished doctoral dissertation, Teachers College, Columbia University, New York.

Kasl, E., Marsick, V. J., & Dechant, K. (in press). Teams as learners: A research-based model of team learning. *Journal of Applied Behavioral Science*.

Kemmis, S. (1988). Action research in retrospect and prospect. In S. Kemmis & R. McTaggart (Eds.), *The action research reader*. Geelong, Australia: Deakin University Press.

Kemmis, S., & McTaggart, R. (Eds.). (1982). *The action research planner*. Geelong, Australia: Deakin University Press.

Lewin, K. (1947). Frontiers in group dynamics. *Human Relations, 1*(2), 150–151.

Lincoln, Y. S., & Guba, E. G. (1985). *Naturalistic inquiry.* Thousand Oaks, CA: Sage.

Merriam, S. (1988). *Case study research in education: A qualitative research.* San Francisco: Jossey-Bass.

Peters, M., & Robinson, V. (1984). The origins and status of action research. *Journal of Applied Behavioral Science, 20*(2), 113–124.

Rowden, R. W. (1995). The role of human resource development in successful small to mid-sized manufacturing businesses: A comparative case study. *Human Resource Development Quarterly, 6*(4), 355–373.

Stake, R. E. (1994). Case studies. In N. K. Denzin & Y. S. Lincoln (Eds.), *Handbook of qualitative research* (pp. 236–247). Thousand Oaks, CA: Sage.

Van Maanen, J. (1988). *Tales of the field: On writing ethnography.* Chicago: University of Chicago Press.

Van Manen, M. (1990). *Researching lived experience: Human science for an action sensitive pedagogy.* Albany: State University of New York Press.

Watkins, K., & Brooks, A. (1994). A framework for using action technologies. In A. Brooks & K. Watkins (Eds.), *The emerging power of action inquiry technologies: New directions in adult and continuing education series* (pp. 99–111). San Francisco: Jossey-Bass.

Whyte, W. F. (Ed.). (1991). *Participatory action research.* Thousand Oaks, CA: Sage.

Yin, R. K. (1984). *Case study research: Design and methods.* Thousand Oaks, CA: Sage.

PART THREE

Getting Started on Research

CHAPTER

Examples of Excellent HRD Research

Gary N. McLean
University of Minnesota

Darlene Russ-Eft
Zenger Miller

As underscored in earlier chapters of this book, finding examples of "excellent" research is not easy. Many decisions must be made by researchers. Both practical and theoretical barriers often impede the researcher from producing the perfect study. None of the articles abstracted in this chapter is an example of "perfect" research; such perfection just does not exist. What we have tried to do, however, is identify excellent human resource development (HRD) articles that represent a variety of professional journals and that cover a broad range of human resource development content fields and research methodologies. It is our judgment that the articles we have chosen are worthy of study both because of the practical value of the findings and recommendations for the practitioner and because they exemplify some aspect of research methodology.

In each instance, we have presented the purpose of the research posed as a question to be answered, the methodology used, the findings, and the recommendations. For readers unfamiliar with statistical analysis, we have provided, in parentheses, very brief explanations of the tests used. All of this takes the form of abstracts paraphrased from the article and occasionally includes brief quotes. Because all research is imperfect in some respect, we conclude each abstract with our unanswered questions, comments, or reservations.

Identification of the articles was one of the most difficult tasks associated with writing this chapter. We frequently disagreed in our reaction to some aspect of the articles and used each other's initial assessment to come to agreement.

Having dealt with the difficult task of selection, we chose not to rank the articles in any way. Therefore, no assumptions should be made about the order in which the abstracts are being presented; they are simply alphabetical by first-listed author. We also have not labeled the methodology used in any of the studies but instead have simply described it. Especially with qualitative research, we found it difficult to fit the articles into one of the commonly accepted methodologies, in part because there does not yet appear to be consensus about what constitutes "appropriate" approaches to specific methodologies but also because many methods used by these authors do not clearly fit into a recognized methodological label.

One other criterion used was how the selected articles contributed to the wide range of topics typically considered to be part of human resource development. As a result, the articles abstracted in this chapter include continuous quality improvement (total quality management), cross-cultural human resource development, performance feedback, organization learning, behavioral modeling, interpersonal-skills training, computer-based interventions, transfer of training, performance prediction, and team building, learning, design, performance, and development.

An abstract can never do justice to the full article or report. For example, every good article will include the theoretical construct underlying the research. This usually involves reference to previous literature. Few abstracts (and none of ours) have room to include such considerations. Likewise, abstracts fail to include the richness of anecdotes that add life and interest to an "excellent" article. For this reason, full bibliographic information is provided for each article to assist readers who wish to access the full text. Readers interested in having a book of excellent articles will find a useful source in the following reference: Russ-Eft, D., Preskill, H., & Sleezer, C. (1996). *Human resource development review: Research and implications*. Thousand Oaks, CA: Sage.

Baldwin, T. T. (1992). Effects of alternative modeling strategies on outcomes of interpersonal-skills training. *Journal of Applied Psychology, 77, 147–154.*

Purpose: What is the impact on reaction, learning, retention, behavioral reproduction, and behavioral generalization of one versus two videotaped model scenarios and of positive only versus both positive and negative behavioral models?

Methodology: A training program on assertive communication was presented to business students, of whom 30 were men and 42 were women. Students were randomly assigned to one of four conditions: (1) one scenario with a positive model, (2) two scenarios with two positive models, (3) one scenario with a positive and a negative model, and (4) two scenarios with a positive and a negative model. To equalize time exposure, students in each condition saw a total of four video showings. The training program covered six learning points about communications and lasted 2.5 hours. Presentation of the learning points was followed by the video models.

Outcomes were assessed through measures of reaction, learning immediately after the training, retention one month after training, behavioral reproduction the same day of training, and behavioral generalization one month after training. After each trainee completed the poststudy questionnaire, he or she was thanked and while leaving the session was approached by a graduate student (a confederate of the researcher). This student indicated that he was raising money for his master's thesis by selling some business publications (whose prices were prohibitively high for students, as shown in pilot testing). This graduate student used a set script of pleas for money. The discussions were audiotaped and later rated by two graduate students blind to condition. The average interrater agreement, or correlation between the two raters, was .92, indicating a high degree of similarity in the ratings.

Findings: A multiple analysis of variance (MANOVA), a statistical test that compares groups on two or more variables including the interaction among the variables, showed that the modeling strategy had a significant effect on the training outcomes. Separate univariate analysis of variance (ANOVAs), a similar test examining one variable at a time, showed that the variability of models had no significant effect on reaction, learning, and retention. The two groups viewing both positive and negative models received significantly lower scores on reproduction and higher scores on behavioral generalization.

Recommendations: Several practical implications emerge from this study. First, behavioral models should be used with the desired outcome in mind. When exact reproduction of skills is desired, then minimal variability should appear in the behavioral models. When, however, generalization of the skills to other situations is desired, then the variability of the behavioral models, including both positive and negative models, is recommended.

Second, this study demonstrated the importance of using multiple measures when examining the outcomes of training. In this case, measures of training reaction, learning, and retention would have yielded no information.

Comments: A pilot test revealed that the student population had low baseline skills in the assertiveness skills being trained. Nevertheless, because this study failed to use pretests of these populations, we do not know whether the differences revealed after training existed among the groups prior to training. In addition, a common criticism of this kind of research is that it is based on a student population, thus limiting generalization of the results. It may be, for example, that the level of intelligence in the student population influenced these findings. In addition, other research suggests that how students perform in an academic setting can be different from how those same students perform similar tasks in the workplace.

Banker, R., Potter, G., & Schroeder, R. (1993). Manufacturing performance reporting for continuous quality improvement [Special issue]. *Management International Review, 33,* 69–85.

Purpose: Does the implementation of continuous quality improvement (CQI) require a shift in management information systems? A secondary question was, To what extent is the information provided to workers on the shop floor about the current status of manufacturing positively related to the implementation of CQI programs?

Methodology: Sixty plants were randomly selected from three industries: electronics, machinery, and auto component suppliers. Forty-two plant managers participated. Managers were interviewed in accounting, production, inventory management, and engineering. Questionnaires were also administered. Plant averages for these questionnaires were based on responses from 3 supervisors and 10 workers. Observations were carried out in 12 plants. Correlation matrices (measuring the shared variance between each set of two variables) were constructed, and regression analysis (a measure of how much each predictor variable contributes to a criterion variable) was run on the criterion variable of how much information was available on the shop floor.

Findings: The correlation matrices indicate significant relationships (at $p < .05$, one-tailed): the number of new products introduced in the last five years and the extent of decentralization are strongly associated with CQI. Decentralization is not related to the number of new products, whereas the length of time involved in CQI is related to CQI, the number of new products, and the extent of decentralization.

The regression analyses revealed that the presence of CQI was the most significant and only consistent predictor (in each case at $p < .05$, one-tailed) of information available (both quality and productivity) and of the presence of charts on the shop floor (for defects, schedule compliance, and machine breakdown).

Recommendations: Implementing CQI principles will increase the amount of information available on the shop floor. Much more research, however, is still needed. The key question is whether there is in fact improvement in quality and productivity as a result of CQI interventions. Further, does the provision of information to the shop floor increase productivity over and above the contributions that accrue from CQI?

Comments: What is not clear from the analysis is whether CQI leads to additional information on the shop floor or whether additional information on the shop floor supports the CQI efforts. Unfortunately, the study design and statistical analyses used do not permit conclusions about cause-effect relationships. Further, none of the variables included in the study focused on the most important variables: actual improvement of quality and productivity. In addition to the unanswered research issues posed by the article's authors, another important question is, Can CQI efforts, absent the shop floor information, have equivalent outcomes in terms of improved quality and productivity?

Bretz, R. D., Jr., & Thompsett, R. E. (1992). Comparing traditional and integrative learning methods in organizational training programs. *Journal of Applied Psychology, 77*(6), 941–951.

Purpose: What are the differential impacts on learning and reaction of the traditional lecture compared with the integrative learning method? "Integrative learning" (or "accelerated learning" or "super learning") relies on the "combination of physical relaxation, mental concentration, guided imagery, suggestive principles, and baroque music" (Druckman & Swets, 1988, p. 6).

Methodology: This study took place at the Technical Educational Resources of Eastman Kodak Company and examined training in manufacturing resource planning. The traditional method was a lecture-based delivery incorporating examples and allowing trainees to ask questions throughout training. The integrative method began with a series of exercises to create a relaxed learning environment. Following facilitator explanation of the concepts, various group discussions, games, stories and poetry, and a business game reinforced the concepts. Trainees presented the concepts in skits or games. Each day ended with the facilitator, accompanied by baroque music, reading a story that incorporated important concepts presented that day.

A Solomon four-group design, which controls for the effects of the pretest, such as expectations and prior learning, resulted in the following groups: (1) a group receiving pretests, integrative training, and posttests; (2) a group receiving pretests, traditional training, and posttests; (3) a group receiving integrative training and posttests only; and (4) a group receiving traditional training and posttests only. A no-treatment control group was also included. The 180 Kodak employees scheduled for manufacturing resource planning training were randomly assigned to the conditions, except for the no-treatment control group, which was obtained through volunteers.

A 40-item multiple-choice test measured performance on the content of the three-day training course. The Faces scale, which consists of a series of faces varying in positive and negative feeling, was modified to obtain reactions to the training. Control measures of cognitive ability, learning-style preferences, affective disposition, and subjective well-being were gathered. Pretest measures of comprehension, reaction, and affective disposition were administered immediately before training. Posttest measures, including all pretest measures along with cognitive ability, learning-style preference, and demographic information, were administered at the end of training.

Findings: A one-way analysis of variance indicated that the integrative, traditional, and no-treatment groups were similar at the pretest. Regression analyses showed that training was the most powerful predictor of performance on the comprehension test. Both trained groups differed significantly from the no-treatment group but were not significantly different from each other. Contrary to prediction, the trainees in the integrative training learned slightly less than did those in traditional training. General cognitive ability and years of formal education were significant predictors of performance but less important than training. Trainees in the integrative sessions had significantly more positive reactions to the training than did those in traditional sessions.

Recommendations: According to expectations, trainees reacted more favorably to the integrative learning method than to the traditional method. Contrary to expectations, however, such positive reactions did not result in improved learning. Integrative learning methods failed to yield superior results in terms of content knowledge. Such a finding suggests that positive or negative reactions to training provide little information as to the outcomes in terms of learning.

Comments: The study results indicate that, based on performance, traditional, lecture-based training is preferred to integrative training. However, the Baldwin (1992) study, previously described in this chapter, suggests several questions to ask of the Bretz and Thompsett study. What impact would the two approaches to training yield in terms of transfer to the job or generalization to other work settings, both of which can be considered performance on the job? Also, what is the retention of this information over time? Perhaps the lecture method yields superior performance immediately after training, but the integrative approach results in better retention of the information.

Another possibility is that there is an interaction effect of training method and training content. For example, technical training may yield the best results with the lecture method, whereas nontechnical training may benefit from the integrative approach. Further research can clarify these issues. Finally, in terms of the present study, random assignment to the no-treatment control group would also have improved the study; it may be that the no-treatment control group comprised superior performers not needing training.

Brooks, A. K. (1994). Power and the production of knowledge: Collective team learning in work organizations. *Human Resource Development Quarterly, 5*(3), 213–235.

Purpose: Why do some teams learn and some not? This study also focused on three collateral questions: (1) What is the team learning process? (2) To what extent do the differences in formal power among individual team members affect the collective team learning outcome of producing useful new knowledge? (3) How do organizational structures and policies affect the team learning process?

Methodology: The study was influenced by an "interpretive interactionist approach" to data collection and analysis in which the researcher tries to understand "how this historical moment universalizes itself in the lives of interaction individuals" (Denzin, 1989, p. 139). This approach was applied to a multiple case study that took place in the research and development unit of a high-technology manufacturing company. Four teams were observed, of which three were considered successful and one unsuccessful. Success was defined by the team's decision about whether to compete in an international, companywide competition for teams.

Given the case study approach, the following tasks were undertaken recurrently or simultaneously: (1) identify the research questions, (2) review the literature, (3) collect personal narratives concerning the teams' learning experience, (4) describe each team and identify elements and features, (5) determine similarities and differences among individuals and teams, (6) code data and identify key themes, (7) assemble and compare data with research questions, (8) reassemble the teams' learning experience to understand it empathetically and in context, (9) locate the teams' learning experience within the historical and social context, and (10) construct the narrative. Data collection included formal interviews with eleven team members, informal discussions with team and organizational members, and eight formal observations of team meetings. Trustworthiness was strengthened by using multiple data sources, two investigators, multiple data collection techniques, negative-case analysis, and critical reflection on the research process.

Findings: Collective team learning seemed to require that team members engage in both active and reflective work. Reflective work tended to occur during team meetings and consisted of posing problems, sharing information, and integrating that shared knowledge. Active work consisted of gathering data from outside the team and disseminating new team knowledge to the organization. Team members with low formal power encountered problems undertaking either reflective or active work. Controlling the power difference among team members led to new knowledge in the technical domain. Removing power differences led to new knowledge in the social domain.

Recommendations: This study reveals that the immediate impact of differences in power among team members and of insufficient formal power for team members led to an inability to control their own time and movement. Such constraints reduced the production of knowledge. Team leaders can address power differences by controlling such differences among team members. For a complete transformation of the organization's culture, however, power differences must be removed. Only then can multiple and divergent perspectives yield enhanced team learning.

Comments: This study presents an excellent example of the case study method. This methodology should be used to examine teams in other organizations to extend understanding of these concepts. The control or removal of power differences may be particularly critical for knowledge production within research and development teams and within high technology manufacturing firms. Expansion to other teams in other environments will illuminate any similarities or differences. In addition, the outcome of team success was defined by the team members themselves. Integrating that internal definition of success with some external definition of success, such as the perspective from higher management or from customers, may reveal other dimensions related to "success."

DiBella, A. J. (1993). The role of assumptions in implementing management practices across cultural boundaries. *Journal of Applied Behavioral Science, 29(3), 311–327.*

Purpose: How does culture affect the process and product of management practices?

Methodology: Three case studies were analyzed "in which management practices were implemented across boundaries of cultural difference" (p. 312). In each instance, two or more cultures were involved (U.S. consultants in Uganda doing strategic planning, U.S. administrators in the Philippines establishing a goal-oriented program, and a structural intervention in India in an international firm). The data were gathered during fieldwork based on a clinical approach. That is, the researcher was involved in interventions in each of the three cases, and the data were a by-product of those interventions. In each instance, cross-cultural conflict emerged based on differing underlying assumptions. Interviews were conducted with key stakeholders and informants representing both cultures. Stories and fables were also used to identify underlying assumptions. The intervention, in each case, was *not* the focus of the research; only the impact of the underlying assumptions on the intervention was studied.

Findings: The result of "swiping" a management practice will differ from initial expectations unless adaptation occurs. In each case analyzed, differing assumptions between the two cultures led to conflict and outcomes that were different from those anticipated prior to the intervention. Further, "activities seen to be rational on the basis of one group's assumptions were labeled irrational or inefficient by the other group" (p. 324). Such assumptions grow out of shared group experiences. "If adaptation does not occur, the greater the chance that the practice will be rejected or impact the innovating system in unintended ways" (p. 325). In the Ugandan strategic planning experience, for example, the U.S. consultants expected the process to take five days, with responsibilities assigned to individual managers working toward achievable ends (goals). The Ugandans, on the other hand, expected to build the process into day-to-day activities (requiring much more calendar time), with responsibility assigned to the team working toward desirable (rather than achievable) ends. Although the specifics differed in the other two cases, the effect of differing assumptions was similarly present.

Recommendations: In any cross-cultural setting, it is essential that the invisible assumptions held by all stakeholders become visible. With identified assumptions, practices can be adapted to fit the assumptions of the recipient client. Discussing such differences between the groups can reduce the anxiety experienced by both groups. Additional research suggested in this article includes the need "to unravel the complex interaction between co-present assumptions existing at multiple levels of analysis" (p. 325) and the identification of the assumptions that cause the greatest conflict when they differ and those that are most resistant to change.

Comments: This article is indicative of the difficulties faced by a participant-researcher, especially in the area of culture. Each researcher has his or her culture that is loaded with invisible assumptions. For example, DiBella made the assumption that, from a U.S. cultural basis, he could adequately and accurately describe another culture. How is it possible to identify one's own assumptions, those of the two groups involved, and the assumptions and culture that exist as the two groups work together? Obviously, it is not, which underscores the importance of the process over the product in such an undertaking. Further, the two groups differed widely in size in two of the three cases. The larger the number, the greater the possibility of introducing heterogeneity, making the task of describing a group as having a single culture increasingly difficult.

Johnson, S. D., & Satchwell, R. E. (1993). The effect of functional flow diagrams on apprentice aircraft mechanics' technical system understanding. *Performance Improvement Quarterly,* **6(4), 73–91.**

Purpose: To what extent can functional flow diagrams aid the initial conceptual learning of technical systems? More specifically, the researchers hypothesized that such flow diagrams will improve "conceptual understanding of technical systems through the development of causal mental models."

Methodology: Eighteen male students in an aircraft systems course in an aviation institute at a university were assigned to either the treatment or control condition. The researchers determined that the two groups were similar in aptitude and domain knowledge through the use of two standardized tests: the American College Testing Program (ACT) examination

and the Survey of Mechanical Insight examination (for aptitude) and grades in prerequisite basic electronic courses (for
domain-specific knowledge).

The training manual used for both groups used "schematic
diagrams to teach about the electrical systems and subsystems of
the King Air 90, 200, and 300 series aircraft" and other major
electrical concepts. The eight students in the treatment condition received a modified training manual. This manual contained
a simplified functional flow diagram prior to displaying the
schematic diagrams. These flow diagrams were verified for content validity by technical experts from two separate institutes.
Tests were developed to measure qualitative understanding of the
system's structure, function, and behavior. Three domain experts
classified the items into the three categories with an interrater
agreement of .91.

During each of four weeks, the students were to complete one
unit of the training manual outside of class. They then received
the unit tests measuring system structure, function, and behavior. In addition, four subjects from each group were randomly selected to complete a card-sorting task assessing conceptual
understanding or knowledge structure.

Findings: Students in the treatment condition displayed superior test performance. A Mann-Whitney U test, a nonparamet-
ric test comparing two groups on their rank, showed significant
differences on behavioral understanding and overall test scores.
MicroQAP, "a microcomputer implementation of generalized
measures of spatial association," correlated subject maps with expert maps. A t-test showed that treatment students created significantly more "expert-like mental models of technical systems"
than did students in the control condition.

Recommendations: The results suggested that use of functional
flow diagrams will lead to greater understanding of technical

systems or at least electrical systems. The authors indicated that such diagrams aid students because (1) they show "only the essential components of the system," (2) they show "meaningful relationships between the concepts and the component parts of a given system," and (3) they "convey the causal nature of the system to the learner." The authors recommended additional research to explore several aspects of the findings: the extent to which training time can be reduced by using such diagrams; the validation and generalization of the findings; the extent to which such diagrams can be further simplified; the use of such diagrams in computer-based instruction; an analysis of the process of developing such diagrams; and the involvement of students in the construction of such diagrams to enhance understanding.

Comments: As the authors themselves recognized, the findings were limited because of the use of students, the use of a single educational institution, the small sample size, and the lack of random assignment of students to groups. Further, the article was not clear about how students were assigned to one of the two groups nor what testing procedures were used. The testing methods revealed students' technical understanding, but such understanding may or may not lead to differences in electrical troubleshooting or problem-solving behavior. The methods described in a later abstract by Rowe and Cooke would provide better information as to the subjects' mental models of such troubleshooting behavior.

McClernon, T. R., & Swanson, R. A. (1995). Team building: An experimental investigation of the effects of computer-based and facilitator-based interventions on work groups. *Human Resource Development Quarterly, 6*(1), 39–58.

Purpose: What are the effects of a computer-based compared with a facilitator-based team-building intervention on a team task among intact work groups?

Methodology: The study examined 24 intact work groups or long-term task forces within a nonprofit organization. These groups varied in size from five to twelve members, with a total of 186 subjects. The design included three treatment conditions and testing at three specified times, plus groups nested within treatments and subjects nested within groups. Effects restricted to a single condition, such as groups that receive only one treatment, are considered to be nested within that condition. The three treatment conditions were (1) a three-hour team-building session, (2) a similar team-building session using a computerized group decision support system, and (3) a no-treatment control. The team-building process included (1) an introduction to team building; (2) data collection, analysis, and feedback using a survey of 12 group dimensions (during which time the computer-supported group used the computer for simultaneous data entry, information processing, and display); (3) discussion of the survey data; (4) brainstorming to create a list of group strengths; (5) brainstorming to develop a list of areas for improvement; and (6) an action plan of ways to improve performance. The three times to take measurements were at the beginning of the first meeting, at the end of the first meeting, and at the end of the next regularly scheduled meeting. For the first measurement time, team members completed a background questionnaire and a measure of group cohesion. The second time, they completed measures of group cohesion, performance, and process. The third time, members completed an assessment of that meeting's group process and group performance outcomes.

Findings: Separate nested analyses of covariance were used to test differences. Cohesiveness of the groups did not differ significantly over time. Solution satisfaction did not differ between the two team-building treatments, but the two treatments produced higher levels of solution satisfaction than the control groups reported. In addition, the team-building treatments differed significantly from the control groups on eight process measures, indicating that the facilitation improved group processes. However, most measures showed no differences among the groups at the third measurement time. Furthermore, most measures indicated decreases over time for the treatment groups as compared with the control groups. The study revealed that one-time team-building interventions have no lasting effect. Furthermore, the addition of computer-supported group decision making did not significantly improve that intervention and had no lasting impact.

Recommendations: This study suggests that such one-time team-building interventions may provide interesting experiences for a team but should not be expected to yield any lasting results. Furthermore, the improved group processes appearing immediately will disappear fairly rapidly.

Comments: Even though organizations regularly invest in one-time interventions, the fact that they have no lasting impact is not surprising. Few one-time interventions without organizational and management support result in long-lasting changes. The level of management support and commitment for these teams was not described in this study. Does a high level of management support enhance these team-building interventions enough to produce positive results? In addition, it would be interesting to determine if repeated use of these team-building interventions has any impact on group process and group outcomes. As a separate comment, the description and interpretation of the findings would be enhanced if the researchers had included the means and standard deviations for each of the measures on each of the groups over time. Furthermore, the use of

T1, T2, and T3 to describe treatment groups rather than time periods was somewhat confusing. One suggestion would be to designate treatment groups (G1, G2, and G3) and time periods (T1, T2, and T3).

❖

Rouiller, J. Z., & Goldstein, I. L. (1993). The relationship between organizational transfer climate and positive transfer of training. *Human Resource Development Quarterly*, 4(4), 377–390.

Purpose: To what extent does organizational transfer climate, separate from learning in training, relate to training transfer and job performance?

Methodology: This study took place within a large, fast food, franchised chain. The trainees, 102 individuals selected to be assistant managers, participated in nine weeks of training. Based on a literature review, workshops with personnel officers, a review by subject matter experts, and a focus group interview with unit managers, a questionnaire was developed to measure organizational transfer climate. These questionnaires, focused on situational cues and on consequences, were completed by two to three managers in each unit just prior to the new trainee's arrival. Training outcomes were measured in terms of learning (throughout the program), transfer behavior (ratings by managers and experienced crew members during the first several weeks on the job), job performance (assessment by the head manager for the unit about eight to twelve weeks after the arrival of the assistant manager), and unit performance (ratings of the entire unit by regional supervisors).

Findings: A multiple regression analysis determined the additional amount of variance contributed by organizational transfer climate after accounting for the relationship of learning and unit performance to transfer behavior. Learning and organizational transfer climate accounted for 54% of the variance in transfer behavior. Further analyses showed that learning is related to transfer behavior, and transfer behavior is then related to later ratings of job performance. In addition, both situational cues and consequences yielded significant effects.

Recommendations: This study provides powerful evidence that the organization and the organizational climate can have positive or negative consequences on the transfer of training. Training the members of the organization in how to provide a supportive environment may be as important as the training itself. Evaluations of training need to take these results into consideration. Rather than merely focusing on the impact of the training event in isolation, evaluations should measure both the training event and the organizational transfer climate.

Comments: The study focused on transfer climate as defined and perceived by the managers of the organization. What happens to these results when examining transfer climate as experienced by the trainees? What happens when transfer is measured by actual job performance factors rather than perceptions of job performance?

Rowe, A. L., & Cooke, N. J. (1995). Measuring mental models: Choosing the right tools for the job. *Human Resource Development Quarterly*, 6(3), 243–255.

Purpose: How do four mental model measures (laddering interview, relatedness ratings, diagraming, and think-aloud) compare on the basis of their ability to predict troubleshooting performance? To what extent can each of the four different mental model measures predict troubleshooting performance? Understanding complex systems and successfully interacting with such systems may require the development of an internal representation or "mental model" of the system.

Methodology: Nineteen technicians in the airborne electronic troubleshooting career field of the Air Force volunteered for the study. The troubleshooting problem concerned the Radar Warning Receiver system on the F-15 aircraft and involved a short-circuited video cable between components of the system. After being given the troubleshooting problem, technicians completed a four-step laddering interview. Then the technician completed a component-relatedness ratings task. This was followed by a diagraming task. Finally, the technician completed verbal troubleshooting, which consisted of troubleshooting actions to be taken, with a subject matter expert responding with the results of those actions. (Note that two subject matter experts independently scored the troubleshooting protocols. Because these were highly correlated, a single performance score was created for each technician by averaging the two scores.) During the verbal troubleshooting task, the technician was asked to express all thoughts verbally. This constituted the think-aloud measure.

Four technicians, with scores one standard deviation greater than the mean, were identified as high performers. An ideal or standard mental model was created from each mental model measure by combining the data from the high performers. The quality of each technician's mental model was assessed in terms of the overlap between the individual's response and the ideal or standard. The resulting knowledge assessment scores were correlated with the performance scores.

Findings: Of the four mental model measures, all but the think-aloud measure predicted performance. Partial correlations revealed that only the relatedness ratings and laddering tasks independently predicted troubleshooting performance. The study demonstrated the importance and validity of mental models in terms of their relationship to performance. Furthermore, the authors found that the mental models of the four experts were different from those of the lower-performing nonexperts.

Recommendations: This research shows that certain mental models are related to troubleshooting performance in the maintenance of complex equipment. Such results suggest that training workers in experts' mental models of equipment may assist in the development of troubleshooting skills. Furthermore, the research indicated that experience and type of mental model are not necessarily correlated with performance. Thus, the human resource practitioner must focus on measures that distinguish experts from novices in terms of performance, if performance improvements are the ultimate goal.

Comments: The description of the results would have been enhanced by the inclusion of some examples of the different models and modeling techniques. The use of volunteers also weakens the impact of the results, because such volunteers may not be representative of the wider population. The research provides a case study of troubleshooting performance in one domain. Further study will be needed to determine if these measures show similar results when used in other domains. In addition, the finding that experts and nonexperts differ qualitatively in their mental models deserves further investigation. For example, when and under what circumstances does an individual's mental model change from that of a novice to that of an expert?

❖

References

Denzin, N. (1989). *Interpretive interactionism*. Thousand Oaks, CA: Sage.
Druckman, D., & Swets, J. A. (1988). *Enhancing human performance*. Washington, DC: National Academy Press.

CHAPTER

9

Finding and Using HRD Research

❖

Catherine M. Sleezer
Oklahoma State University

James H. Sleezer
Data Systems Services

Publications that address the learning and performance needs of individuals, work groups, and organizations have become a growth industry. In the current information boom, human resource development (HRD) professionals can find so many potentially applicable articles that sorting through them to find the "good stuff" can seem like a daunting task. To make the task easier, this chapter identifies major sources of HRD research literature, profiles the top five research journals in HRD, describes a process for accessing HRD research on specific topics, and

Note: The authors gratefully acknowledge the contributions of Jill Hough in reviewing this chapter.

suggests strategies for getting the most from research articles. To set the stage for this information, the next section overviews definitions for the term *HRD*.

Definitions of HRD

During its short history, the domain of HRD has grown dramatically. For example, Gilley and Eggland (1989) noted that HRD during the past two decades has emerged as a professional field in its own right. Jacobs (1990) pointed out that "HRD constitutes a unique body of knowledge and research derived from more fundamental disciplines" (p. 66), and in 1991 Watkins and Willis defined HRD as a field of study and practice. These views, when integrated, reveal that HRD is a professional field of study and practice with its own unique body of knowledge and research.

However, the literature contains many definitions for HRD. For example, Nadler and Nadler (1989) defined HRD as "organized learning experiences in a given period of time to bring about the possibility of performance change and/or personal growth" (p. 4). McLagan (1989) defined it as the "integrated use of training and development, organization development, and career development to improve individual, group, and organization effectiveness" (p. 7). Watkins' (1989) definition was "the field of study and practice responsible for the fostering of a long-term, work-related learning capacity at the individual, group, and organizational levels. As such it includes—but is not limited to—training, career development, and organization development" (p. 427). Finally, Swanson (1994) defined HRD as a process of developing and/or unleashing human expertise through organization development and personnel training and development for the purpose of improving performance.

Although these definitions contribute to understanding the field, they vary in focus, purpose, and outcomes. Further, none operationalize the concept of HRD at a level of specificity needed to identify major sources of research literature. For example, each would be a poor filter for determining whether a team study conducted in a university graduate class should be classified as HRD or as not-HRD.

The following definition, which we have developed, is useful for culling HRD research from other literature:

> Human resource development is the study and practice of human interactions in organizations including interactions with processes, tools, systems, other humans, or even the self. HRD encompasses knowledge, skill, and value bases. The goal of HRD is to understand the interactions, processes, and systems and to ultimately support and improve individual, process, and organizational learning and performance. Operationally, this definition delimits HRD in five ways: (1) its focus is on understanding, unleashing, or facilitating the use of human expertise within organizations; (2) it occurs within one or more business, industry, military, or public-sector organizations but does not include educational institutions; (3) it focuses on individuals who are already connected with an organization; (4) it focuses on adults and their learning and work; and (5) it is limited to the preparation of HRD professionals and characteristics of interactions, systems, processes, programs, instruments, and their components or results.

The operationalized definition of HRD provides a foundation for this chapter. Based on this definition, a "team" study conducted in a university graduate class would be labeled as not-HRD because it fails to focus on individuals who are already in the organization.

Major Sources of HRD Research Literature

HRD research literature is comprised of scientific works. As Dorelan (1988) pointed out, scientific works provide a foundation for a discipline and its specialties. Fox (cited in Dorelan, 1988) noted that publication is central to research productivity to such a degree that work becomes *a work* only when it is published. Further, as Dorelan stated, "a substantial portion of scientific work is published in professional journals, the set of which can be viewed as a central institution of science" (p. 79).

HRD practitioners and scholars can benefit from knowing which journals publish a substantial portion of the field's scientific work. Anyone who has recently tried to access information using traditional strategies (e.g., by glancing at a friend's bookshelf, reading a practitioner journal, or dropping into the library to see what's new) knows what we're talking about here. Even a cursory search reveals myriad HRD books and articles that purport relevance for practitioners and scholars. However, quality is an issue. The days when you could believe it if it was in writing are long gone. Your friend's bookshelf and the practitioner journals are just as likely to turn up "sounds good" but "doesn't work" information. Also, an unsystematic library search is little better because the scholarly and nonscholarly, high-quality and low-quality, and HRD and non-HRD materials are all mixed together. Knowing the key scholarly journals in the field provides a leg up in any search for quality HRD literature.

This is not a trivial benefit. A study by Sleezer, Sleezer, and Pace (1996) identified 1,290 refereed HRD articles published in

258 distinct journals from 1980 to 1994. Each article "fit" the operationalized definition of HRD; was abstracted in the Educational Resources Information Center (ERIC), Abstracted Business Inform (ABI/Inform), or PsycLit database; and was identified with a database search that used the term *research* combined with one of the following terms: *human resource development, human resource, training, management development, organization development,* or *career development.*

Table 9.1 provides a macroview of HRD research sources. It shows that although many journals publish HRD-related research, fewer core journals exist.

Table 9.2 lists the journals that published at least fifteen articles in the time period 1980 through 1994 and in the time period 1990 through 1994. Five journals listed in the table have been in existence for less than fifteen years: *Human Resource Development Quarterly* was first published in 1990; *Performance Improvement Quarterly* and *Journal of Organizational Behavior* were first published in 1988; *Public Administration Quarterly* and *Organization Development Journal* were first published in 1983. In addition, one journal, *Management Education and Development,* ceased publication in 1993 and one journal, *Group and Organization Studies,* changed its name to *Group & Organization Studies* (articles published under both titles are included in the table).

**Table 9.1. Number of Refereed HRD
Research Articles from 1980–1994 Across Journals**

Number of Articles Published	Number of Journals
At least 15 articles	18
Between 10 and 14 articles	10
Between 5 and 9 articles	40
Between 2 and 4 articlse	81
1 article	109

Table 9.2. Journals That Published Fifteen or More HRD Research Articles from 1980–1994

Journal	Number of HRD Research-Related Articles Published 1990–1994	Number of HRD Research-Related Articles Published 1980–1994
Human Resource Development Quarterly	23	23
Public Personnel Management	15	45
Performance Improvement Quarterly	14	16
Journal of Organizational Behavior	12	12
Personnel Psychology	12	74
Journal of Applied Psychology	10	15
Journal of Management	10	31
Management Education and Development	10	19
Public Administration Quarterly	10	16
Academy of Management Journal	9	44
Management Decision	9	19
European Journal of Operational Research	8	24
Organization Development Journal	8	22
Human Relations	7	38
Academy of Management Review	6	54
R and D Management	5	19
Group and Organization Studies/Group & Organization Studies	3	43
Journal of Applied Behavioral Science	2	24

Profiles of the Top Five
HRD Research Literature Sources

HRD professionals who know the focus and characteristics of key journals can most efficiently access needed information. This section overviews the top five journals based on the number of HRD research articles published during the 1990–1994 period.

1. *Human Resource Development Quarterly (HRDQ)*. This journal publishes scholarly work that addresses the theoretical foundations of HRD, HRD research, and evaluation of HRD practices. The *HRDQ* recognizes the interdisciplinary nature of the HRD field and brings together relevant research from related fields, such as economics, education, management, and psychology. It provides an important link in the application of theory and research to HRD practice. It is sponsored by the Academy of Human Resource Development and the American Society for Training and Development.

2. *Public Personnel Management*. Directed toward professionals in the public personnel field, each issue of this journal contains in-depth articles on the latest issues in the field. Recent articles have focused on such topics as workforce diversity, family and medical leave legislation, stress reduction, career stage training, drug testing, sexual harassment, benefits, and assessment. A strength of the journal is the wide variety of research and views expressed by the diverse body of authors appearing each quarter. Contributors include human resource practitioners, public administration educators, and public personnel consultants. The journal is published by the International Personnel Management Association (IPMA), a nonprofit membership association for public personnel professionals.

3. *Performance Improvement Quarterly (PIQ)*. The goal of this journal is to advance the discipline of performance technology and to stimulate professional discussion in the field through the publication of scholarly works. Performance technology is a set of methods and processes for solving problems and realizing opportunities related to the performance of individuals, small groups, and large organizations. The journal emphasizes original work involving technologies such as front-end analysis or evaluation and interventions such as motivation, personnel selection, instruction, ergonomics, or guidance. It is sponsored by the International Society for Performance Improvement.

4. *Journal of Organizational Behavior*. This journal's aim is to report and review the research in the industrial/organizational psychology and organizational behavior fields throughout the world. It focuses on research and theory in all topics associated with occupational/organizational behavior including motivation, work performance, selection, training, organizational change, research methodology in occupational/organizational behavior, employment, job analysis, behavioral aspects of industrial relations, managerial behavior, organizational structure and climate, leadership, and power.

5. *Personnel Psychology*. This journal publishes empirical applied research that deals with a wide range of personnel problems facing public and private sector organizations. Articles focus on aspects of personnel psychology that include employee selection, training and development, job analysis, productivity improvement programs, work attitudes, labor-management relations, and compensation and reward systems. The journal also regularly publishes reviews of the research literature in these areas.

Although each of the top five sources for HRD research has carved a unique niche for providing scholarly information, overlaps among the journals do exist. This knowledge is useful when trying to identify information relative to specific issues.

A Process for Accessing HRD Research

Although yesterday's textbooks and favorite practitioner journals contain interesting insights, they are insufficient for the HRD professional who must face today's triple-prong challenge of dynamic work environments, an exploding information base, and the high visibility that results from HRD's critical impact on individual, group, and organization performance. Meeting the challenge requires access to systematic studies and scholarly discourse. Access to much of this material can be gained through CD-ROM databases.

CD-ROM databases have been available since about 1985. Prior to that time, computer database searches involved examining data that was stored on mainframes. The cost of a search was often based on the number of citations retrieved or how long the search actually took to complete. With the advent of personal computers and CD-ROMs, cost is seldom a factor. Today, searching for research is less costly and easier than ever before. Three particularly useful CD-ROM databases for HRD research are PsycLit, ABI/Inform, and ERIC.

Electronic databases are usually indexed with categories similar to a library's card catalog: author, title, and subject. Also, most of them have an added capability—key word searching—that you can use to identify citations that contain selected words in the title, authors' names, subject descriptors, or abstracts.

Many strategies are available for using these databases to find the information that you want. The strategy that will work best depends on your background knowledge and your personal preferences. Searching a database is a personal experience that reflects the combination of skill, luck, imagination, and curiosity (Jack, 1985).

One useful strategy for starting a search is to *go with what you know*. For instance, if you know the title or author of a work highly relevant to the topic, start the search by keying in that information. Use the resulting citation, abstract, and subject categories to identify additional references, useful subject descriptors, and appropriate key words. You may also want to obtain articles that are cited in order to review their references.

Another strategy is to *go with what you think you know*. CD-ROM databases usually have a subject descriptor guide or thesaurus for identifying subject categories that might be appropriate for your search. Scanning this resource can give you some known terms. Try one! Or try a key word search using a subject that you think might exist. The challenge is to choose the right word or words. Because you select the words and see the results almost immediately, you can control the process. If you get too many citations, narrow the search by adding another key word or two; if you get too few citations, try a broader key word. Many databases treat a series of key words as separate searches. That is, searching for the term *human resource development* is really three searches, one for *human*, one for *resource*, and one for *development*. The results of the three searches are combined, providing you with the records common to all three searches. Additionally, most databases will let you indicate when two words must appear together. For instance, in some databases inserting the abbreviation *adj* between key terms assures that the terms are adjacent to one another in the abstract or title. In other databases, you enclose a multiword term in quotation marks.

But remember, the search will identify only the citations that include your key word (or words) in the abstract or title of the work. If you get even one useful citation, you are on your way. Examine that citation to see what subject descriptors were used to classify it; look for some key words relevant to your topic. This process of obtaining a few fairly suitable citations and adding to the initial set by retrieving more items using those subject descriptors has been referred to as *pearl culturing* (Jack, 1985).

Yet another strategy is to *go for help*. Asking an experienced librarian for assistance has two major advantages. First, most librarians are familiar with the databases available at their locations and can help you choose those appropriate for your search. Second, they usually have experience in using the databases and can help you identify some good subject descriptors or key words. If the first librarian you ask cannot help, get a second opinion from another librarian who may be more familiar with the topic area.

Avoid limiting your searches to only the databases that index HRD research. If your study focuses on a particular business or industry, consider using databases that index research in those areas. Also, remember, not all works are indexed on the electronic databases. To do a thorough search of the literature, you may need to use additional avenues such as print indexes and the actual journal issues.

Strategies for Getting the Most from Research Articles

After you find research articles on the topic, then what? The task of efficiently distilling and integrating the pertinent information from the articles can seem overwhelming—especially for HRD professionals who have little research experience. Quickly skimming the articles you found will probably reveal some that are easy to read and entertaining, some that have interesting abstracts but are written in unintelligible jargon, and some that are only marginally connected to your topic. Also, if you have done a good search, you will find some that appear to be "right on target." You might even find one article that provides an overview of the topic. This section provides three practical strategies for making some sense of what you have.

1. *Use article sections to quickly find the information you need.* Instead of reading an entire article from start to finish, use a search strategy. Most research articles include five sections: abstract, introduction, methodology, results, conclusions. Start with the abstract. It provides an overview of the article and usually contains one or more sentences that describe each of the other sections. The abstract should give you an idea of whether the article will be useful. If it seems too far afield, set it aside; you can always come back to it later if you decide it fits your needs. If reading the abstract suggests that the article is relevant, read the introduction. It should explain why the topic is important and how this article connects to other work in the field. Next, examine the conclusion. It presents what the author learned from the study. One or more of these sections may be sufficient for your purposes.

HRD professionals who are more expert in research and a specific topic are likely to find the methodology and results sections to be of interest. These sections detail the systematic process that was used to study the topic and the outcomes that resulted. If an article seems to be particularly important, you will want to examine the methodology and results sections thoroughly, but a quick glance will probably be sufficient for the first review of the articles.

2. *Use a circular rather than a linear process.* Some people expect to thoroughly read one source, find all of its key points, and

then move on to the next source, never to return to the first. However, because people construct knowledge differently, a more useful strategy might be a circular approach that involves revisiting sources as you gain additional information.

For example, you can start by skimming the easier-to-read articles. Notice any terms or concepts that the author defined. See if you can identify a key point or two. Writing them down may help. Next, browse articles that overview the topic. These readings integrate information from multiple sources, so check out the articles' section headings to learn how the author organized the topic. Again, notice any terms that are defined. Check the references to see if any of your other sources are cited or if there are other interesting sources that you should access. As you advance to more complex articles, look back at points that may have been raised in articles you read earlier in the process. An article you read later in the process may give you better insight into one you read earlier.

3. *Identify key points in each article and compare them.* When you are accessing multiple sources, the task of remembering who wrote what can be difficult. It can be even more difficult to master the areas of agreement and disagreement among articles. This strategy can help you overcome such difficulties. Use your own words to identify key points in each article. Write them down. Look for agreement and/or disagreement among authors. A useful comparison tool is a two-axis matrix that lists article titles on one axis and the key points on the other axis. The sample two-axis matrix shown in Table 9.3 demonstrates how a comparison of four articles might be structured. This comparison focuses on HRD definitions. As this example highlights, comparisons across works can highlight similarities and differences in the works.

Table 9.3. Sample Two-Axis Matrix Comparing Key Points of Publications

Author(s)	Expected outcome of HRD	Components of HRD			
		Training and Development	Career Development	Organization Development	Other
McLagan (1989)	Improve individual, group, and organization effectiveness	X	X	X	
Watkins (1989)	Foster a long-term, work-related learning capacity at the individual, group, and organizational levels	X	X	X	Not limited to the first three components, but not specified
Swanson (1994)	Improve performance at the organization, process, and individual levels	X		X	Performance improvement
Nadler & Nadler (1989)	Possibility of performance change and/or personal growth				Not clear

Conclusion

This chapter provides a snapshot of HRD work, a list of core refereed journals that publish HRD research articles, a profile of the top five journals, a process for accessing research, and some strategies for getting the most from research articles. Although obtaining quality HRD research is a challenge, it is needed by all HRD professionals to give new perspectives on (1) yesterday's heuristics; (2) idealized visions of what should be; or (3) values, practices, and research specific to other fields and contexts. With the ability to efficiently access research, today's HRD professionals are positioned to base their practice on knowledge gained from systematic study of HRD efforts and work systems— and to make even stronger contributions to workplace learning and performance.

References

Dorelan, P. (1988). Testing structural-equivalence hypotheses in a network of geographical journals. *Journal of the American Society for Information Science, 39*(2), 79–85.

Gilley, J. W., & Eggland, S. A. (1989). *Principles of human resource development*. San Francisco: Jossey-Bass.

Jack, R. F. (1985, December). Meatball searching: The adversarial approach to online information retrieval. *Database, 8*(2), 45–52.

Jacobs, R. L (1990). Human resource development in an interdisciplinary body of knowledge. *Human Resource Development Quarterly, 1*(1), 65–71.

McLagan, P. (1989). *Models for HRD practice*. Alexandria, VA: American Society for Training and Development.

Nadler, L., & Nadler, Z. (1989). *Developing human resources*. San Francisco: Jossey-Bass.

Sleezer, C. M., Sleezer, J. H., & Pace, R. W. (1996). Identifying core journals for HRD research: Process and results. *Proceedings of the Academy of Human Resource Development Conference*. Austin, TX: Academy of Human Resource Development.

Swanson, R. A. (1994, June). *Human resource development: Performance is the key*. Keynote address presented at the 3rd International Interdisciplinary Conference of the International Research Network for Training and Development, University of Milan, Italy.

Watkins, K. (1989). Business and industry. In S. Merriam & P. Cunningham (Eds.), *Handbook of Adult and Continuing Education*. San Francisco: Jossey-Bass.

Watkins, K. E., & Willis, V. J. (1991). Theoretical foundations of models for HRD practice—A critique. In N. M. Dixon & J. Henkelman (Eds.), *Models for HRD practice: The academic guide*. Alexandria, VA: American Society for Training and Development.

CHAPTER

10

Ways of Seeing
Disciplinary Bases of Research in HRD

David L. Passmore
Pennsylvania State University

This closing chapter argues first that understanding, using, and conducting research in HRD requires seeing research problems through disciplinary bases. Then it provides précis of three of the disciplinary bases that guide research in HRD: economics, general systems theory, and psychology.

Why discuss disciplinary bases? First, a discipline provides a way of seeing problems, issues, and opportunities in HRD that has broadly understood and accepted theoretical and empirical underpinnings. All HRD researchers and the research they produce is

Note: I gratefully acknowledge the editorial advice and assistance of Maureen L. Passmore in the preparation of this chapter.

199

influenced by disciplinary bases, whether they are explicitly acknowledged or not. Many of the debates among researchers can
be traced to different disciplinary-based ways of seeing HRD
problems. Practitioners using research need to recognize disciplinary influences when considering research findings and applications. Second, every practitioner faces pressures that stem from
these discipline bases. For example, CEOs may place pressure on
 HRD to increase profits (economics) while employees want HRD
to provide learning that improves their performance and satisfaction (psychology). Third, cultivating this way of seeing is a
linchpin in the development of a professional practice of HRD.
Like other applied fields of study and practice, HRD must ground
itself in disciplinary bases.

❖

Need for a Disciplinary Basis for HRD Research

Although a tendency toward monastic devotion is not a prerequisite, the research process requires attention, deep and true, to
both substance and process, and it is often best served when
niceties are foregone and the angle of pursuit is blunt.

Even so, research is a human act, not a rigid, assigned process;
strange how many people look on it primarily as rule-following!
Take a recipe for, say, instrument development, research design, or
evaluation, stir well with statistical techniques, cook the mixture
in a computer, and offer the result on a platter according to guidelines provided by some publication manual. To be sure, rules have
their place. Without them, rigor has no benchmark. Still, the rules
tell little about the adventure of the HRD research process.

Indeed, research in HRD can be an adventure. Of course, this
type of adventure is not the same type as portrayed in a swash-
buckling, high-seas saga. It is the kind of adventure that artists

experience when they accept serendipity and synthesize, integrate, and look beyond the experience at hand. The research process can also provide mysticism and wonder and ecstasy. The ability to see the world from a unique perspective is not merely a badge of individuality or a cultivated eccentricity; in fact, in HRD research, that ability is essential because HRD is an emerging field of study still dominated by practice, in need of discovering and documenting its disciplinary basis.

A discipline is a body of knowledge with its own organizing concepts, codified knowledge, epistemological approaches, undergirding theories, particular methodologies, and technical jargon. Academics view it as a specific body of teachable knowledge with its own background of education, training, procedures, methods, and content areas (Mayville, 1978, p. 9). A discipline is the foundation upon which practice rests or from which it is developed (Schein, 1973, p. 43), providing the structure necessary for common effort to solve common problems through common communication among researchers. It unifies and provides continuity for research and practice.

Professional knowledge, according to Schein (1973, p. 39), has three components: (1) an underlying discipline or basic science; (2) applied science or engineering; and (3) skills and attitudes that foster service to a client. Schön's seminal work (1983) provided examples of the many facets of knowledge that professionals must apply in their work beyond formal disciplinary-based knowledge. Without the formal propositional knowledge (when I change A, B also changes) that comprises the theoretical foundation of a discipline, the basis for practice becomes little more than superstition. Superstitious beliefs leave the field of practice open to hucksters, fads, and appeals to authority, all of which seem to influence the adoption of innovations in HRD practice more than in many other fields, unfortunately.

The history of HRD appears to be a road map of the wax and wane of gimmicks. Surely we are tired of spending our time, effort, and money on superstition. Not only is following superstition costly but another consequence is the eventual loss of respect for the field of practice among its constituents. No matter how long it takes, someone eventually musters the courage to say that the emperor is naked. No wonder so many HRD professionals are such cynics. The practice of HRD had its origins in needs for applications and solutions, not in theory. Most of its practitioners are devoted to the penultimate aim of organizational effectiveness, not to furthering discipline-based knowledge (although, as mentioned, that could occur along the way). As characterized by Gilbert (1978), the field of HRD has focused on engineering human behavior in organizations, not on the science that enables it.

Three Disciplinary Views for HRD Research

Three disciplinary bases, three ways of seeing, have been suggested as being the foundation of HRD research (Swanson, 1996) and are reviewed in this section: (1) economics; (2) general systems theory; and (3) psychology. The stock of knowledge defining these fields is vast. As a result, no attempt is made to be exhaustive. As any brief expedition through literature indexes will reveal, human resource development issues are viewed through many disciplines, not just these three. For example, evolutionary theory is used to characterize the life cycle of organizations in one line of research (see, e.g., Aldrich & Mueller, 1982). Researchers in HRD need to appreciate and cultivate a sense of disciplinary knowledge particular to HRD problems, issues, and opportunities.

Economics

Almost all resources are scarce, even if they seem available without cost. We are beginning to realize that seemingly free resources, such as pure air and water, are limited. Even dirt, which might be freely available in its original location, is a limited resource if it is transported to a new location for use. People and societies seek to satisfy their needs and desires with the available resources. However, full satisfaction is impossible, except for ascetics and the very wealthy, because human needs and desires are limitless and resources are constrained. The view in mainstream economics is that scarcity is pervasive.

Economics is the study of the allocation of scarce resources among unlimited and competing uses. For the most part, economics does not examine what uses are worthy (essentially a normative question of ethics and morals), although assumptions, explicit or implicit, about proper goals to pursue underlie most economic analyses. Rather, economics examines what uses are chosen (essentially a scientific question) without regard to the personal or social values undergirding the choice. As you might imagine, the so-called positivist epistemological stance of mainstream economics that purports to examine what people do, as opposed to what they ought to do, is controversial inside and outside the field of economics.

Economics considers two main issues. The first is how to allocate scarce resources. This issue drives the branch of economics called *microeconomics*. Microeconomics concerns itself with production and consumption choices made by the lowest common denominators of economic activity: firms, households, individuals. In fact, the English word *economics* is derived from the Greek word *oikonomika*, which now would be translated as *household management*. The second issue addressed by economics is how to achieve full use of scarce resources. This issue motivates the branch of economics called *macroeconomics*, which focuses on relationships among such aggregates as output, income, employment, expenditure, or interest rates.

Microeconomics and macroeconomics concern themselves with questions about the quantity and quality of goods that are produced and consumed. The methodological playing field for economics is the market, in which the quantity and quality of goods supplied and demanded are regulated by their price. Economic inquiry largely involves analysis of factors that affect supply, demand, and price of goods. Economic goods can take material form (e.g., oranges, steel, Chevrolets), and money often is used as a measure of prices.

The analytical power of economics is magnified by broadly expanding the notion of economic goods to include intangibles (e.g., altruism) that are scarce. Some goods (e.g., children) are not priced in the market. To the economist, though, everything involves choices and indeed has a price. The price of one good can be measured by opportunities foregone for consumption of another good. For example, the opportunity cost of a child is the income foregone by the child's caretaker, who might otherwise be working for pay. The price of each hour of leisure is the income lost from an hour of work. The employer's price for an employee's absence from work is the value of foregone production.

A major assumption in economics is that the goal of economic activity is to maximize utility, a construct embracing all of the satisfactions realized through consumption, production, and related behavior. Under dictatorship, the dictator's utility is maximized. The slave owner's utility is maximized in a slave society. In a free society, individuals maximize their individual utility, however they define it. Economics is not so much concerned about the components of utility as with the fact that individuals bundle their satisfiers differently. Uncovering the components of utility is left to psychologists or market researchers. Belief that economic actors attempt to maximize their utility is sufficient for economic theory.

The discipline of economics has seen application to research in HRD along many strands. Economic methodologies originally developed to weigh the costs and benefits of public projects and policies have been adapted to forecast and evaluate the feasibility and net effects of HRD strategies and interventions. However, human capital is perhaps the economic concept that has attained the most currency in research and general discussions about the role and worth of HRD. Human capital is the capacity of human beings to produce goods and services. Its analog is physical capital, which includes residential and nonresidential structures and producers' durable equipment with productive capacity. Just as individuals, firms, and societies can invest in the creation and maintenance of physical capital, investments also are made in human capital. Investors in physical and human capital expect to earn a return on their investments. Accordingly, decisions about investments in physical as well as human capital can rely on calculations of net present value, discounted lifetime earnings, or similar investment criteria. Although there is some resistance to conceptualizing human productive capacity alongside the productive capacity of structures and machines, the analogy between physical and human capital is quite rich. It provides a direct link between investments in health and education and expected benefits to the economy. It allows consideration of HRD strategies and interventions alongside non-HRD solutions. It uses a lexicon of investment that is quite familiar to decision makers who already ponder, say, infrastructure or money market investments using the same criteria.

Interestingly, researchers who identify themselves with HRD infrequently view their research problems through the lens of economics. Economic research that affects HRD policy almost always is conducted by economists, mainly in think tanks, universities, and research institutes far removed from HRD practice. For instance, the National Bureau of Economic Research has published a quite visible line of research on training investments in the private sector. This research, which contains some simple, naive, and inane definitions of participation in training, has marched by largely unnoticed by the HRD community. Clearly, HRD researchers and practitioners have not sufficiently embraced economics as a basis for research and practice in ways that could benefit organizations and the HRD field.

General Systems Theory

A system is an arrangement of elements that forms an organic whole. A system is organic in the sense that is resembles a living organism. As such, a system has interdependencies among its elements. Although a systematic viewpoint often has a functional focus (e.g., separate analyses of physiological systems might occur from the point of view of, say, circulatory, digestive, or excretory functions), the aim of a systems analysis is to capture the interrelated and complex nature of the phenomenon under study.

The relationships among elements of a system are lawful (i.e., determined, dependable). Elements directly or indirectly affect one another. Moreover, a system communicates with its environment. It affects and is affected by external forces and systems. Most important for science progress, previously unknown deductions about system behavior are possible by knowing the nature of relationships of system elements among themselves and with the environment. For this reason, study of systems can bear fruit for applications in fields of practice.

General systems theory, or GST, is a collection of general concepts, principles, tools, problems, and methods associated with systems of any kind. GST is considered by some to be a discipline in its own right, with a framework for analysis, synthesis, identification, and optimization of systems. More properly, though, GST is more akin to a research direction than a discipline because it actually aims to integrate diverse content areas and disciplines by means of a unified approach. Applications of GST have occurred in business, chemistry, cybernetics, economics, education, engineering, environmental science, health, manufacturing, organizational studies, physics, and sociology, to name a few subjects (Stowell, West, & Howell, 1993).

GST evolved only recently, most notably with the writings of von Bertalanffy (1956). However, forces brewed centuries before led to the development of GST. On one hand, physics turned mathematical in the eighteenth century. Derivation of the theorems of theoretical mechanics allowed deduction of new knowledge from first principles without the need for observation and experimentation. Enthusiasm peaked for the hope that all aspects of the physical world were strictly determined and therefore eventually specifiable mathematically. The result, after derivation of mathematical structures, would be a universe totally within the prediction and control of humans. The physicists wanted to derive systems that leave, to use Mackay's (1974) phrase, "nothing buttery." Biology, on the other hand, was a descriptive science during the eighteenth century. Biologists considered life, the fundamental subject matter of biology, to operate in an altogether unique manner apart from any other physical laws. That biology is reducible to the same laws that govern physics (the very hope of physicists) seemed absurd to most biologists. Then came the crunch. When the laws of thermodynamics were discovered and chemistry matured in the mid-nineteenth century, the boundaries between biology and physics began to collapse. Laws of conservation of matter and energy were applied to living organisms.

Many other advances began to reduce knowledge thought to be unique to specific disciplines to common truths. As years passed, much progress was made to render chemistry down to key physical laws, and, in general, scientific concepts have become more interchangeable among disciplines. For instance, biological and social theories are becoming fused. Links are drawn between concepts in meteorology and sociology.

Yet controversy remains about the validity of the GST approach. As an example, opponents of GST point to the fact that all life phenomena have not been reduced to fundamental chemistry and physics. Even if GST ultimately is not successful in reducing the world to a small set of connected concepts, its success is best measured by the degree that it has fostered interdisciplinary insight. GST has lead to greater sympathy for aims to replace older, analytic, atomic technique in science with a more holistic approach to complex problems.

GST contributes to the solution of problems by placing them in a general structural context abstracted from specific content. Such an approach forces the analyst to research a problem in depth and to integrate it in breadth, instead of pursuing the topic in depth and in isolation. Specialization is the original sin that GST attempts to purge.

In response, GST pursues at least four aims in its missionary work (Cavallo, 1979). First, GST seeks to investigate the similarity of laws, concepts, and models from various fields and to help in useful transfers from one field to another. Second, it encourages development of adequate theoretical models in fields lacking them. Third, it minimizes duplication of theoretical effort in different fields. And fourth, it improves communication among specialists by providing integrated scientific language, supplying what economist Kenneth Boulding (1956) called the skeleton of science upon which the articulate contents of science can hang.

The touchstone of the GST approach is the search for isomorphisms among seemingly disparate systems. An isomorphism is a mathematical similarity that exists when a one-to-one correspondence exists among the elements of systems and when the relationships among the individual system elements are the same in the systems. That is not to say that the systems are strictly identical. Isomorphism exists if systems essentially have the same structure, but they do not need to share the same specific content. The big payoff of this feature, of course, is the possibility of simultaneous deduction of postulates about the behavior of the systems. The trick is to find and expose isomorphic systems. In this way, concepts and phenomena from one field of investigation are compellingly translated into those of another, and common deductions are possible. Bingo. The world is a little smaller, and additional integrative research is stimulated. von Bertalanffy (1957) provides an interesting example of deductions that are possible from isomorphic properties of growth in such diverse systems as biological cells, living populations, or even modern corporations.

Systems theory is increasingly visible in HRD theory and practice. Gilbert's (1978) human competence model is based on systems theory as is Rummler and Brache's (1995) model and several models of organizational change. The trend toward performance consulting as an operating philosophy also has its roots in systems theory. The notion that organizations have multiple performance levels (organization, process, individual) is a major contribution of systems theory. Systems theory provides practitioners with a means to understand and intervene more effectively in organizations, which are complex systems. By rejecting the notion of simple unidimensional solutions to organizational performance problems, general systems theory makes possible more significant gains in performance.

Research supporting HRD could benefit from the general analogical approach taken by GST. Productive advancement of the field could occur by looking for strong parallels between existing systems and HRD systems. In addition, systems thinking involves a certain rigor that might add useful structure to HRD systems. For instance, some training actually can be viewed as a closed system beginning with goals and incorporating feedback and knowledge of results. The system involves a process for moving trainees from an initial state to a target state. GST principles for system optimization might provide an alternative to general instructional systems design approaches commonly employed.

Psychology

One thing is for certain: psychology is the science of behavior and mental processes of humans and other animals. Beyond that, we have something that resembles a teenager's closet. Psychology encompasses many subfields that focus on specific aspects of behavior and mental life. To name a few: experimental, personality, social, industrial-organizational, clinical, counseling, community, development, and quantitative.

Psychological inquiry is guided by many perspectives. A biological approach is taken to examine how physiological processes shape behavior and mental processes. An evolutionary approach holds that behavior is the result of evolution through natural selection. The behavioral approach emphasizes the role of learning. How people take in, mentally represent, and store information and integrate this information into behavior is the subject matter of the cognitive approach. The humanistic approach emphasizes each person's quest for autonomy, growth, and release of innate potential for good. The psychodynamic approach examines the internal struggle between social restrictions and impulses to satisfy instincts and wishes.

Psychology was once described as having a long past but only a short history. Originally, psychology was philosophy. Plato gave center stage to the difference between mind and body. Aristotle wrote extensively on memory, motivation, and emotion, and he offered a concept of the mind as a blank wax tablet on which experience is written. René Descartes helped establish empiricism, that is, that knowledge comes from observing nature. British empiricists (among others, Hobbes, Locke, Hume) forged the philosophical underpinnings of modern psychology. In the middle of the nineteenth century, the physiologist Helmholtz calculated the speed of neural impulses, and the psychophysicist Fechner quantified the relationship between stimulus intensity and sensation to establish the possibility of measuring and experimenting upon psychological phenomena and processes. In 1879, Wilhelm Wundt created a psychological laboratory in Germany to study the science of experience through introspection and self-observation.

Dissatisfaction with the self as the unit of analysis led to emergence of other movements in psychology. Associationists believed that human beings know by means of the senses and that complex ideas are built from association with simpler ideas. Functionalists studied the role of the mind in adapting the organism to its environment. Behaviorists focused solely on observable links between stimuli and responses and discarded concepts such as the mind and consciousness. Gestalt psychologists refreshed interest in mental processes by asserting that behavior is irreducible to simple sensations and elements. Along the way, psychoanalysis enjoyed popular appeal by focusing almost entirely on the origin, development, and treatment of abnormal behavior.

Modern psychology retains this mix of approaches and emphases, while it has branched out rapidly to diverse areas of application that include art, religion, law, human factors engineering, consumer behavior, and forensic medicine. However, the major unifying theme of psychology is its continuing focus on behavior and mental processes. If anything, the recent history of psychology has seen more complete reliance on empirical research as a hallmark for scientific progress.

Unlike economics or GST, psychology is a discipline that already has a strong hold on HRD practice. Issues related to promotion of human learning, assessment of human skills, knowledge, and attitudes, the role of motivation and rewards in eliciting performance, and the design of work environments all involve psychological concepts, methodology, and insights. The psychological perspective is particularly appropriate for research focused on individual human performance issues. Much of traditional HRD practice (particularly training) emerged from the psychological discipline. Although psychological theory is still invaluable to HRD practice, it has become increasingly apparent that it is necessary to integrate economics and general systems theory perspectives for effective HRD practice.

Conclusion

The three disciplines reviewed in this chapter are candidates, among many others, for enriching research that supports HRD practice. HRD requires discipline-based knowledge in order to develop the professional knowledge to perform successfully as a field of practice. Successful research in HRD requires a successful melding of the needs of HRD practice with discipline-based knowledge.

It should be apparent that the three disciplines, when taken separately, would lead researchers and practitioners to different solutions to organizational effectiveness. A psychological approach might focus on enhancing learning, motivation, or personal responsibility. An economic approach might lead to enlarged or long-term investments or a demand for short-term profits. A systems perspective might point to a combination of process and strategic change in light of economic and personnel issues. All could be right—and wrong. Thus the need for researchers and practitioners to understand disciplinary-based ways of seeing.

The unique contribution of HRD in organizations may, in fact, be its ability to integrate these three disciplinary bases to improve organizational effectiveness. Standing alone, each of them may be myopic. When applied in combination, and to appropriate needs, they are powerful. By combining these three (and perhaps others) in a systematic field of study and practice, HRD attains its uniqueness.

References

Aldrich, H. E., & Mueller, S. (1982). The evolution of organizational forms. In B. M. Staw & L. L. Cummings (Eds.), *Research in organizational behavior* (pp. 33–87). Greenwich, CT: JAI Press.

Becker, G. S. (1960). Economic analysis of fertility. In *National Bureau of Economic Research: Demographic and economic change in developed countries* (pp. 209–231). Princeton, NJ: Princeton University Press.

Boulding, K. E. (1956). General system theory: The skeleton of science. *General Systems, 1*, 11–17.

Cavallo, R. E. (Ed.). (1979). Systems research movement: Characteristics, accomplishments, and current developments [Special issue]. *General Systems Bulletin, 9.*

Gilbert, H. (1978). *Human competence: Engineering worthy performance.* New York: McGraw-Hill.

Mackay, D. (1974). *The clockwork image.* Downers Grove, IL: Inter-Varsity Press.

Mayville, W. V. (1978). *Interdisciplinary: The mutable paradigm.* Washington, DC: American Association for Higher Education. (AAHE-ERIC/Higher Education Research Report No. 9)

Rummler, G., & Brache, A. (1995). *Improving performance: How to manage the white space on the organization chart*. San Francisco: Jossey-Bass.

Schein, E. (1973). *Professional education*. New York: McGraw-Hill.

Schön, D. A. (1983). *The reflective practitioner: How professionals think in action*. New York: Basic Books.

Stowell, F. A., West, D., & Howell, J. G. (Eds.). (1993). *Systems science: Addressing global issues*. New York: Plenum Press.

Swanson, R. A. (1996). Human resource development: Performance is the key. *Human Resource Development Quarterly, 6*(2), 207–213.

von Bertalanffy, L. (1956). General system theory. *General Systems, 1*, 1–10.

von Bertalanffy, L. (1957). Quantitative laws in metabolism and growth. *Quarterly Review of Biology, 32*, 217–231.

INDEX

A

Abstracted Business Inform (ABI/
Inform), 187, 191
Academy of Human Resource Devel-
opment, 18, 189
Action research: case study method
in, 147–153; defined, 11–12,
148–149; process of, 11–12, 34
Aldrich, H. E., 202, 213
Alternative modeling strategies, study
of, 163–165
American Society for Training and
Development, 189; Research
Committee of, 19
Analysis of covariance (ANCOVA),
81
Analysis of variance (ANOVA), 80–81

Apply research, and value chain, 25,
34–36, 44
Argumentation, for synthesis,
109–110
Argyris, C., 109, 111, 148, 150, 154n,
155
Aristotle, 211
Ary, D., 70, 86
Atheoretical HRD practice, 4–10

B

Baldwin, T. T., 21, 34, 35, 45, 50, 61,
163–165, 169
Banker, R., 165–167
Barnum, D. T., 47, 60
Becker, G. S., 213
Becker, H. S., 143, 155

Beer, M., 127, 135
Behavioral event interview technique (BEIT), 154n
Bereiter, C., 3, 19, 124, 135
Bobko, P., 70, 86, 87
Borg, W. R., 87
Boulding, K. E., 127, 135, 208, 213
Brache, A. P., 123, 137, 209, 214
Bretz, R. D., Jr., 167–170
Brooks, A. K., 113, 134, 135, 146, 153, 155, 157, 170–172
Burke, W. W., 119, 120n, 135
Burnett, M. F., 65
Business results, 36–40

C

Campbell, D. T., 87
Campbell, J. P., 116, 124, 135
Capability measures, 39
Carnevale, A., 48, 60
Case study research: aspects of, 138–157; background on, 138–139; bounding, 142–143; data analysis for, 144–145; data collection for, 143–144; defined, 138; focus and assumptions for, 140–141; guidelines for, 153–155; illustrated, 147–153; literature review for, 141–142; procedures for, 139–147; rigor in, 146–147; in theory building, 126, 130–132, 143; types of, 131–132, 139
Categorical data, 72–74
Causal-comparative research, purpose of, 70
Causality, 84–85
Cavallo, R. E., 208, 213
Certainty, degree of, in quantitative research, 67–68
Change, planned, theories of, 119–123
Chein, I., 148, 150, 155
Chi, M.T.H., 124, 135
Climate, for transfer of learning, 34–35, 179–180

Cohen, L., 113, 140, 156
Cohen, S. L., 36, 46
Collaboration as professional partnership, 47–61
Comparative study, as tool, 80–82
Conclusions, in qualitative research, 104–106
Construct validity, 75–76
Content validity, 75
Context, for transfer of learning, 34–36
Continuous or interval data, 73–74
Continuous quality improvement, study of, 165–167
Contracts, for collaborations, 56
Control group design, 77
Cook, S., 148, 150, 155
Cooke, N. J., 176, 180–182
Copeland, T. E., 40, 45
Corbin, J., 126, 133, 137
Core competencies, and Focus research, 30–31
Cormier, W. H., 87
Correlational research, purpose of, 70
Correlations, interpreting, 81–82
Criterion validity, 75
Critical incident technique, 153–154
Cross-cultural management study, 172–174
Culture: surveys of, 100
Cummings, T. G., 54, 61

D

Databases, 18, 191–193
D'Aveni, R., 45
Dechant, K., 140, 141, 143, 156
Denzin, N. A., 88, 91, 111, 141, 143, 144, 156, 170, 182
Descartes, R., 211
Descriptive research: purpose of, 70; as tool, 79–80
Design decisions, 76–78
Development, in research cycle, 12, 15–16

Dewey, J., 140
Diagnosis, and planned change, 121, 122
DiBella, A. J., 172–174
Dichotomy, for synthesis, 109
Disciplinary bases: aspects of, 199–214; background on, 199–200; conclusion on, 212–213; economics as, 203–206; foundational, 202–212; general systems theory as, 206–210; need for, 200–202; psychology as, 210–212
Discipline, defined, 201
Dixon, N. M., 9, 19
Dorelan, P., 186, 197
Druckman, D., 167, 182
Dubin, R., 115, 125, 129, 136
Dulebohn, J. H., 47, 60

E

Eastman Kodak Company, Technical Educational Resources of, 167–170
Economic Value Added (EVA), 40–41
Economics, as disciplinary base for HRD, 203–206
Educational Resources Information Center (ERIC) Clearinghouse, 18, 187, 191
Effective research, characteristics, 26–28
Eggland, S. A., 184, 197
Einstein, A., 114
Eisenhardt, K. M., 126, 130, 132, 136
Elden, M., 150, 156
Elmes, M. B., 93, 112, 142, 156
Evaluation: atheoretical four-level model, 9; and planned change, 121–122; and theory, 117–118
Events network, for synthesis, 108–109
Experimental research, purpose of, 69
Explanatory studies, as tool, 84–85

F

Factor analysis, 76
Factorial ANOVA, 81
Farr, M. J., 124, 135
Feedback, 33
Ferris, G. R., 47, 60
Flanagan, J. C., 113, 154n, 156
Flowchart, for synthesis, 108
Focus groups, 98
Focus of research, and value chain, 25, 28–32, 43
Ford, J. K., 34, 45
Freese, L., 125, 136
French, W., 119, 120n, 136
Frequencies tool, 79
Functional flow diagrams study, 174–176

G

Gainer, L. J., 48, 60
Galagan, P. A., 23, 45
Gall, M. D., 87
Gavan, C., 143n, 156
General systems theory (GST), as disciplinary base for HRD, 206–210
Generalization: analytic, 130; in quantitative research, 67–68
Gersick, C. J., 154, 156
Gielen, E., 9, 20
Gilbert, H., 202, 209, 213
Gilbert, T. F., 123, 127, 136
Gilley, J. W., 184, 197
Glaser, B., 113, 133, 136, 142n, 144, 154, 156
Glaser, R., 124, 135
Goldstein, I. L., 34–35, 46, 179–180
Gradous, D. B., 13, 20, 36, 46, 136
Graphic models, for synthesis, 110–111
Grounded theory: and case studies, 154; in theory building, 126, 132–133
Guba, E. G., 113, 137, 141n, 144, 147, 156, 157

H

Hackman, J. R., 91–92, 112
Hammer, M., 122, 136
Hansen, C. D., 92, 112, 144, 155
Harding, J., 148, 150, 155
Held, M., 48, 61
Herzberg, F., 136
Hobbes, T., 211
Holland, S. L., 48, 60
Holleran, L. P., 47, 60
Holton, E. F., III, 9, 20, 36, 45, 65, 134, 136
Hough, J., 183n
Howell, J. G., 207, 214
Huberman, A. M., 89n, 90n, 104–105, 112
Huck, S. W., 87
Human resource development: defined, 184–186; journals on, 187–191; theories underlying, 133–134. *See also* Research
Human Resource Development Quarterly (HRDQ), 170, 176, 179, 180, 187, 188, 189
Hume, D., 211
Hunter, J. E., 36, 46

I

Impact of research, 38
Implementation, and planned change, 121, 122
Integrative learning methods study, 167–170
International Personnel Management Association (IPMA), 189
International Society for Performance Improvement, 190
Interpersonal skills training outcomes and study, 163–165
Interpretation: in case studies, 145–147; in quantitative research, 85–86; and theory, 117, 118
Interviews, in qualitative research, 96–98

J

Jack, R. F., 192, 193, 197
Jacobs, L. C., 70, 86
Jacobs, R. L., 47, 48, 54, 61, 127, 134, 136, 184, 197
John, S., 143n, 156
Johnson, S. D., 174–176
Journal of Applied Behavioral Science, 172
Journal of Applied Psychology, 163, 167
Journal of Organizational Behavior, 187, 188, 190
Journals, on human resource development research, 187–191

K

Kahn, R. L., 127, 137
Kahnweiler, W. M., 92, 112, 144, 156
Kaplan, A., 125, 126, 136
Kasl, E., 140, 141, 143, 156
Kasouf, C. J., 93, 112, 142, 156
Katz, D., 127, 136
Kavanaugh, M. J., 35, 46
Kearns, D., 23
Kemmis, S., 148, 149, 156
Kerlinger, F. N., 87
Kirkpatrick, D. L., 9, 20, 36, 45
Knowledge: growth of, by intention or extension, 126–127; professional, 201
Koller, T., 40, 45
Kotter, J. P., 119, 120n, 123, 136
Krueger, R. A., 98, 112
Kuhn, T. S., 13, 20, 125, 137

L

Lanseth, R. W., 20
Lawler, E. E., 54, 61, 137
Learning research, and value chain, 25, 32–34, 43–44
LeCompte, M. D., 137
Ledford, E. L., Jr., 32, 46
Ledford, G. E., 54, 61
Leimbach, M. P., 21, 36, 46, 47, 50, 61
Levin, M., 150, 156

Lewin, K., 113, 119, 120n, 137, 148, 152–153, 157
Lincoln, Y. S., 88, 91, 111, 113, 137, 141, 143, 144, 147, 156, 157
Locke, J., 211

M

Mackay, D., 207, 213
Magjuka, R. J., 34, 35, 45
Manion, L., 113, 140, 156
Marsick, V. J., 88, 92, 112, 134, 137, 138, 140, 141, 143, 156
Mayville, W. V., 201, 213
McCall, M. W., 70, 86
McClernon, T. R., 20, 176–179
McCloy, R. A., 124, 135
McLagan, P., 184, 196, 197
McLean, G. N., 100, 112, 161
McTaggart, R., 148, 149, 156
Measures: mental model, 180–182; tools for, 73–76; of variables, 72–78
Merriam, S., 140, 157
Methods: aspects of, 63–157; case study, 138–157; qualitative, 88–113; quantitative, 65–87; selecting, 72–78; theory-building, 114–137
Miles, M. B., 89n, 90n, 104–105, 112
Mills, G. E., 54, 61
Mohrman, A. M., 54, 61
Mohrman, S. A., 54, 61
Morical, K. E., 36, 46
Mueller, S., 202, 213
Multiple analysis of variance (MANOVA), 81
Multiple regression tool, 82–83
Murrin, J., 40, 45

N

Nadler, L., 184, 196, 197
Nadler, Z., 184, 196, 197
National Bureau of Economic Research, 206

Naturalism, in theory building, 125–126, 130–133
Newstrom, J. W., 9, 20
Newton, I., 114
Nicholas, S., 20
Nonexperimental research, purpose of, 69–70

O

Observation, in qualitative research, 100–102
Oppler, S. H., 124, 135
Ordinal or rank order data, 73–74
Organization records, in qualitative research, 102–103
Organizational strategy, and value chain, 24–25, 29–31, 43
Oxford, E., 143n

P

Pace, R. W., 54, 61, 186–187, 198
Participants: in action research, 150–151; in quantitative research, 71–72
Partnership and collaborative research: aspects of, 47–61; background on, 47–48; conclusion on, 60; as formal process, 56–57; guidelines for, 52–58; implications of, 58–60; long-term, 57–58; as partnerships, 48–52; purposes of, 49, 51; research in all, 53–54; as service agreements, 50–51
Partnership research concept, 54
Passmore, D. L., 4, 13, 20, 199
Passmore, M. L., 199n
Patterson, C. K., 137
Patton, M. Q., 95, 101, 112
Pearl, K., 36, 46
Performance Improvement Quarterly (PIQ), 174, 187, 188, 190
Performance research, and value chain, 25, 36–41, 44
Personnel Psychology, 188, 190
Peters, M., 149, 157

Plato, 210–211
Poole, M. S., 32, 46
Population, determining, 71
Porter, M., 24, 46
Positivism, in theory building, 125, 126–129, 130
Potter, G., 165–167
Practice: in research cycle, 15, 16; research integrated with, 47–61; research questions derived from, 54–55; shaped by theory, 119–123
Predictive studies, as tool, 83–84
Preissle, J., 137
Preskill, H., 163
Pre-test design, 77
Priorities, and theory, 118
Problems, and theory, 117
Psychology, as disciplinary base for HRD, 210–212
PsycLit database, 187, 191
Public Personnel Management, 188, 189

Q

Qualitative research: appropriateness of, 92–94; aspects of, 88–113; and case studies, 131; conclusion on, 111; data analysis in, 103–111; data collection for, 96–103; data synthesis in, 106–111; defined, 88; nature of, 89–95; process of, 94–95; quantitative research compared with, 90; themes of, 95; value of, 90–92
Quality, in quantitative research, 66–68
Quantitative research: aspects of, 65–87; background on, 65–66; conclusion on, 86; interpretation in, 85–86; method selection for, 72–78; participants in, 71–72; process for, 68–86; qualitative research compared with, 90; quality in, 66–68; question formulation for, 69–71; statistical analysis tools for, 78–85; strengths of, 66

Quasi-experimental research, purpose of, 70
Question formulation, 69–71
Questionnaires, in qualitative research, 99–100

R

Ralphs, L. T., 27, 46
Rapoport, A., 127, 137
Razavieh, A., 70, 86
RCA, and research, 51–52
Readiness, and planned change, 120–121, 122
Reality, emergent, 90–91
Reengineering, and planned change, 122–123
Reflection, for synthesis, 107
Regression tool, 82–83
Reliability, of measures, 74–75
Research: aspects of, 3–20; in collaborations and partnerships, 53–54; commitment to, 7–8; customer-driven, 26–27; cycle of, 13–17, 31–32; databases on, 191–193; directions for, and theory, 118–119; disciplinary bases of, 199–214; domains of, 9, 14–16; and economics, 205–206; examples of excellent, 161–82; expectations for, 55–56; finding and using, 183–198; and general systems theory, 209–210; help with, 18–19; importance of, 1–61; initiating, 159–214; literature sources on, 186–191; methods for, 63–157; and outcomes, 6; for practitioners, 15, 16, 47–61, 197; and psychology, 212; reporting, 17–18; rigor of, 28, 49, 146–147; strategies for using, 193–196; time frames for, 27, 31–32; and value chain, 21–46
Research definition, 10–11
Research process, 11–17
Research, purpose of, 3–4, 21–23, 66

Return on investment: 36–37, 39–40; and collaborations, 51–52
Robinson, D. G., 26, 46
Robinson, J. C., 26, 46
Robinson, V., 149, 157
Rogers, J., 143n
Rosen, S. D., 47, 61
Rossett, A., 22, 46
Rouillier, J. Z., 34–35, 46, 179–180
Rowden, R. W., 92, 112, 144, 157
Rowe, A. L., 176, 180–182
Rummler, G. A., 123, 137, 209, 214
Russ-Eft, D., 161, 163

S

Sager, C. E., 124, 135
Samples, choosing random, 71–72
Satchwell, R. E., 174–176
Sauquet, A., 143n
Sawzin, S., 36, 46
Sayre, S., 16, 20
Scales, valid, 76
Scardamalia, M., 3, 19, 124, 135
Schein, E., 201, 214
Schmidt, F. L., 36, 46
Schön, D. A., 148, 150, 154n, 155, 201, 214
Schroeder, R., 165–167
Schuster, J. R., 32, 46
Scriven, M., 91, 112
Service agreements, collaborations as, 50–51
Sharp, and research, 52
Shephard, P., 143n
Sheppeck, M. A., 36, 46
Significance of results, 85–86
Sleezer, C. M., 100, 112, 163, 183, 186–187, 198
Sleezer, J. H., 183, 186–187, 198
Smith, H., 51, 6
Smith, P. C., 54, 61
Snow, R. E., 125, 127–128, 137
Stake, R. E., 126, 130, 131–132, 137, 139, 140, 146, 157
Standard deviation tool, 80

Stanley, J. C., 87
Stanton, S. A., 122, 136
Statistical analysis tools, 78–85
Stephan, E., 27, 46
Stowell, F. A., 207, 214
Strauss, A., 113, 126, 133, 136, 137, 142n, 144, 154, 156
Swanson, B. L., 88, 93, 112
Swanson, R. A., 3, 10, 12, 13, 20, 36, 46, 97, 100, 106, 112, 113, 134, 137, 176–179, 184, 196, 198, 202, 214
Swets, J. A., 167, 182

T

Tannenbaum, S. I., 35, 46
Team building study, 176–179
Team learning studies, 140–141, 143, 146, 170–172
Tesch, R., 89n
Theory: defined, 115; on human resource development, 133–134; importance of, 115–116; of planned change, 119–123; in research cycle, 15, 16–17; roles of, 116–119
Theory building: aspects of, 114–137; background on, 114–115; case study research for, 130–132, 143; grounded theory in, 132–133; methods of, 125–133; phases of, 129; positivism in, 126–129; process of, 123–125; summary on, 135
Theory-practice link: ix–xi, xiii, 4–5, 9–10, 22–23, 47–48
Thompsett, R. E., 167–170
Three-axis matrix, 107–108
Time frames, 27, 31–32
Time series design, 77–78
Torraco, R. J., 17, 20, 114, 134, 137
Tracey, J. B., 35, 46
Transfer of learning: and Apply research, 34–36; climate for, 34–35, 179–180
t-test tool, 80
Two-axis matrix, 107

U

U.S. Air Force, 181–182
U.S. Army Air Force, 154n

V

Validity, of measures, 74–76
Value chain: areas of, 25, 28–41; aspects of, 21–46; case study of, 41–44; conclusion on, 45; described, 23–26
Van Maanen, J., 113, 146, 157
Van Manen, M., 113, 142n, 157
Variables: dependent and independent, 72, 74, 81; measures of, 72–78
Villet, J., 48, 60
von Bertalanffy, L., 123, 127, 137, 207, 209, 214

W

Walton, E., 127, 135

Watkins, K. E.

Watkins, K. E., 88, 113, 134, 137, 138, 153, 157, 184, 196, 198
Weick, K. E., 124, 125, 128–129, 137
West, D., 207, 214
Whetten, D. A., 137
Whyte, W. F., 148, 157
Wilensky, A. S., 92, 112, 144, 156
Willis, V. J., 184, 198
Wundt, W., 211

X

Xerox Corporation: action research at, 150; and value chain, 23

Y

Yin, R. K., 113, 126, 130–131, 132, 137, 138, 140, 146, 157

Z

Zingheim, P. K., 32, 46

THE AUTHORS

Timothy T. Baldwin, Ph.D., is Dow Teaching Fellow and associate professor of management at the Indiana University Graduate School of Business. Baldwin received his B.A., M.B.A., and Ph.D. degrees in human resource management from Michigan State University. His research has focused on effective human resource management, particularly within the area of training and development. A prolific writer, he has published his research work in leading academic and professional outlets such as *Journal of Applied Psychology, Personnel Psychology, Academy of Management Journal, Training and Development Journal,* and *Human Resource Development Quarterly.* Baldwin has won several national research awards, including three from the National Academy of

Management, and has twice been the recipient of the Richard A. Swanson Excellence in Research Award presented by the American Society for Training and Development (ASTD).

Graduate School of Business, Indiana University, 10th and Fee Lane, Suite 650, Bloomington, IN 47405, 812-855-0221

Michael F. Burnett, Ph.D., is professor of vocational education and director of the School of Vocational Education at Louisiana State University (LSU). During his sixteen years as a member of the faculty at LSU, he has been active in both the undergraduate and graduate teaching programs, the school's research program, and service activities at the community, state, and national levels. More recently, Burnett's activities have centered around the school's graduate programs, in which he teaches the research design and methodology courses. He received his Ph.D. degree from the Ohio State University.

School of Vocational Education, Louisiana State University, Baton Rouge, LA 70803, 504-388-5748

Elwood F. Holton III, Ed.D., is associate professor of human resource development at the Louisiana State University School of Vocational Education, where he also coordinates the degree programs in HRD. His research focuses on analysis and evaluation of organizational performance systems. He is also the president-elect of the Academy of Human Resource Development. In addition to publishing numerous journal and professional articles, Holton is coeditor of *Conducting Needs Assessment* (American Society for Training and Development, 1995), editor of the forthcoming case book *Leading Change in Organizations* (American Society for Training and Development, in press), and coauthor (with Malcolm Knowles) of the forthcoming *The Adult Learner: A Neglected Species*, 5th edition (Gulf Publishing, in press). He received his B.S. degree in business and his M.B.A. and Ed.D. degrees in human resource development, all from Virginia Tech.

School of Vocational Education, Louisiana State University, Baton Rouge, LA 70803, 504-388-2456.

Ronald L. Jacobs, Ph.D., is associate professor and section head, Workforce Education and Lifelong Learning, the Ohio State University. He serves as associate editor of *Human Resource Development Quarterly* and will assume the editorship for volume nine. He also serves as vice president for research of the Academy of Human Resource Development. Jacobs is a frequent contributor to the human resource development literature and has presented his research at numerous groups nationally and internationally. He is the recipient of the Richard A. Swanson Award for Excellence in Research and the Scholar of the Year Award (1995), Academy of Human Resource Development. Much of his scholarly writings have focused on the relationship between theory and practice, with the intent of encouraging greater involvement of researchers in practice situations. Jacobs' 1995 book (with Michael Jones) is titled *Structured on-the-Job Training: Unleashing Employee Expertise in the Workplace.* He received his Ph.D. degree from Indiana University.

Workforce Education and Lifelong Learning, The Ohio State University, 287 Arps Hall, Columbus, OH 43210, 614-292-0581

Michael P. Leimbach, Ph.D., is director of research for Wilson Learning Corporation. Leimbach provides leadership for the research capability in the areas of measurement, concept research, and evaluation. Since joining Wilson Learning in 1984, he has developed measurement systems in sales, leadership, and organizational development; has managed major concept development research studies in sales effectiveness, collaborative work structures, and performance management; and has also developed Wilson Learning's program evaluation capability, program evaluation system, Return-on-Investment model, and the program evaluation guides for Wilson Learning's brand products. Leimbach received his Ph.D. degree in developmental psychology from the University of Minnesota. He has published numerous professional articles and has made presentations for a wide range of professional organizations. He has also been an adjunct faculty member for the University of Minnesota, the College of St. Catherine, Augsburg College, and Fairview-Deaconess Hospital.

Wilson Learning Research and Development, 7500 Flying Cloud Drive, Eden Prairie, MN 55344, 612-828-8645

Victoria J. Marsick, Ph.D., is associate professor of adult and continuing education at Columbia University, Teachers College, and is chair of the Department of Higher and Adult Education. Prior to joining Teachers College, she was a training director at the United Nations Children's Fund. She holds a Ph.D. degree in adult education from the University of California, Berkeley, and an M.P.A. degree in international public administration. Marsick currently consults with both the private and public sectors on the design of learning organizations, action reflection learning, and training approaches. She is an associate of Partners for the Learning Organization and of Leadership in International Management, chairs the research committee of the American Society for Training and Development, and is a member of the board of the Academy for Human Resource Development. Her most recent book is titled *In Action: Creating the Learning Organization* (1996, with Karen Watkins).

Teachers College, Columbia University, New York, NY 10027, 212-678-3754

Gary N. McLean, Ed.D., is professor and coordinator of human resource development and adult education at the University of Minnesota, St. Paul. He has been an independent consultant, primarily in training, organization development, and quality transformation, for over twenty-five years, serving as principal consultant with ECCO (Effecting Creative Change in Organizations). He currently teaches courses in organization development, management development, quality and productivity improvement, and international human resource development. He is a frequent speaker and has written almost a hundred journal articles and twenty textbooks. McLean is editor of the *Human Resource Development Quarterly* and consulting editor for the *Journal of Education for Business*. He has received numerous recognitions for his teaching, research, and service. He graduated from Graceland College in pre-commerce; the University of Western Ontario (B.A. in business administration); Teachers College, Columbia University, in business education (M.A. and Ed.D.); and United Theological Seminary (M.Div.).

Human Resource Development, 1954 Buford Avenue,
University of Minnesota, St. Paul, MN 55108, 612-624-4901

David L. Passmore, Ph.D., lives in State College, Pennsylvania, where he is professor of education at Pennsylvania State University. He also is senior scientist in the Center for Trade, Technology, and Economic Growth, a unit in Penn State's intercollege Institute for Policy Research and Evaluation. Passmore is 1996–97 Visiting Scholar of the University Council on Vocational Education. He has been a member of graduate faculties of the University of Massachusetts at Amherst and the University of Northern Iowa and has coordinated research on the economic consequences of deafness as senior research associate for the National Technical

Institute for the Deaf. Passmore also served for one year as Carnegie Visiting Scholar in Maternal and Child Health with the Injury Research Center of the Harvard School of Public Health. He earned his Ph.D. degree in education from the University of Minnesota in 1974 and focuses his research on planning and evaluating education for employment.

305D Orvis Keller Building, Pennsylvania State University, University Park, PA 16802, 814-863-2583

Darlene Russ-Eft, Ph.D., is division director of research services at Zenger Miller, an international consulting, training, and education company headquartered in San Jose, California. Her responsibilities include managing the company's market and product research activities as well as consulting with clients about methods for measuring the effectiveness of consulting and training. In addition, she is the author or coauthor of articles and essays about research issues that have appeared in major journals. She also is a frequent speaker at regional, national, and international psychology and training association meetings. She is the immediate past chair of the research committee of the American Society for Training and Development and has recently been elected to the board of the American Evaluation Association. Russ-Eft received a 1996 Editor of the Year award from Times Mirror for her research work. She received her Ph.D. degree in experimental psychology from the University of Michigan.

Research Services Division, Zenger Miller, Inc., 1735 Technology Drive, San Jose, CA 95110, 408-452-1244

Catherine M. Sleezer, Ph.D., is assistant professor of human resource development at Oklahoma State University. She conducts research and teaches graduate courses in human resource development. In addition, her presentations and published works focus on using HRD research and theory to improve the practice of workplace learning and performance. Sleezer also works with organizations to improve training and performance. The many projects that she has successfully completed range from analyzing training needs for Oklahoma judges, to helping decision makers in manufacturing plants implement performance improvement systems, to evaluating human performance needs related to new services and technology. She received her Ph.D in human resource development from the University of Minnesota.

Human Resource Development, School of Occupational and Adult Education, Oklahoma State University, Stillwater, OK 74078, 405-744-9197

James H. Sleezer, M.B.A., works in Computing and Information Services at Oklahoma State University. He is also an independent consultant, serving as principal consultant with Data Systems Services. He has completed graduate work in database management, research, and telecommunications management. His presentations and publications focus on using technology to support performance improvement. He received his M.B.A degree from the University of Minnesota.

Data Systems Services, 823 Oakridge Drive, Stillwater, OK 74074, 405-372-9189

Barbara L. Swanson, Ph.D., is senior partner of Swanson & Associates, Inc., a consulting firm in St. Paul, Minnesota, specializing in expertise for performance improvement. She is an expert in assisting senior executives plan and implement strategies for the improvement and management of organizational performance, work process performance, and job level performance. Swanson's broad background also includes conducting organizational needs assessments and the design, development, and evaluation of training programs. She received her Ph.D. degree from the University of Minnesota with a research focus on managing and assessing the implementation of change in organizations. Swanson has published a number of journal articles and given numerous presentations related to quality improvement. She has completed study trips to Japan, Germany, the Netherlands, the United Kingdom, and South Africa for the purpose of studying quality improvement, organization development, and training practices in those nations.

Swanson & Associates, Inc., 168 E. 6th Street, Suite 4002, St. Paul, MN 55101, 612-292-0448

Richard A. Swanson, Ed.D., is professor of human resource development and director of the HRD Research Center at the University of Minnesota. He is also senior partner of Swanson & Associates, Inc., a consulting firm specializing in expertise for performance improvement. Swanson has more than 180 publications on the subjects of performance and human resource development. He served as the founding editor of the *Human Resource Development Quarterly* and is presently serving as the president of the Academy of Human Resource Development. His 1994 book, *Analysis for Improving Performance,* received the outstanding book awards from the International Society for Performance Improvement and the Society for Human Resource Management. Swanson received his doctorate from the University of Illinois.

Human Resource Development, University of Minnesota, 1954 Buford Avenue, St. Paul, MN 55108, 612-624-9727

Richard J. Torraco, Ph.D., is assistant professor of human resource development, University of Nebraska-Lincoln. Torraco holds a B.S. degree from the University of Massachusetts, an M.S. degree from Boston University, and a Ph.D. degree in human resource development from the University of Minnesota. His expertise includes the strategic alignment of the human resource function to the organizational mission, business processes, and job performance demands of dynamic business and industrial settings. His recent article "The Strategic Roles of Human Resource Development" was selected by *Human Resource Planning* as the feature manuscript for volume 18, number 4. Torraco is presently consulting in the areas of performance improvement and workforce expertise. He is editor of the *Academy of Human Resource Development Conference Proceedings* for 1997 and 1998 and is serving as chair of the 1997 HRD Performance Pre-Conference.

Human Resource Development, University of Nebraska, 3125 Cedar Avenue, Lincoln, NE 68502, 402-472-3853

Karen E. Watkins, Ph.D., is professor of adult education at the University of Georgia and director, graduate programs in human resource and organizational development. She is the author, with Victoria Marsick, of *Creating the Learning Organization* (American Society for Training and Development Press, 1996), *Sculpting the Learning Organization: Lessons in the Art and Science of Systemic Change* (Jossey-Bass, 1993), and *Informal and Incidental Learning in the Workplace* (Routledge, 1990). Watkins is the author of more than fifty articles and chapters and two additional books in the areas of human resource and organizational development. She is the immediate past president of the Academy of Human Resource Development. Her most recent research and consultation activities have included learning organization projects with Ford Motor Company, Nortel, Inc., and Mariott Hotels. Watkins received her Ph.D. degree from the University of Texas at Austin.

Department of Adult Education, University of Georgia at Athens, 404 Tucker Hall, Athens, GA 30602, 706-542-4355

Human Resource Development Research Handbook Sponsors

The Academy of Human Resource Development

The Academy of Human Resource Development (AHRD) is a global organization made up of, governed by, and created for the human resource development (HRD) scholarly community of academics and reflective practitioners. The Academy was formed to encourage systematic study of HRD theories, processes, and practices; to disseminate information about HRD; to encourage the application of HRD research findings; and to provide opportunities for social interaction among individuals with scholarly and professional interests in HRD, from multiple disciplines and from across the globe.

> The Academy of Human Resource Development
> P.O. Box 25113
> Baton Rouge, LA 70894–5113
> U.S.A.
> Phone: 504–334–1874   Fax: 504–334–1875
> E-mail: office@ahrd.org   Website: http://www.ahrd.org

The American Society for Training and Development

The American Society for Training and Development (ASTD) was founded in 1944 and is the world's largest professional association in the field of workplace learning and performance. The Society provides research, analysis, and practical information derived from its own research, the knowledge and experience of its 58,000 worldwide members, its conferences and publications, and the coalitions and partnerships it has built through research and policy work.

> The American Society for Training and Development
> 1640 King Street
> Box 1443
> Alexandria, VA 22313–2043
> U.S.A.
> Phone: 703–683–8100   Fax: 703–683–8103
> Website: http://www.astd.org

Other leading-edge business books from Berrett-Koehler Publishers

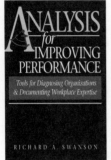

Analysis for Improving Performance
Tools for Diagnosing Organizations and Documenting Workplace Expertise

Richard A. Swanson

*A*NALYSIS FOR *IMPROVING PERFORMANCE* details the front-end work essential to the success of any performance improvement effort. In clear language and easy-to-follow steps, Swanson shows how to do the rigorous preparatory analysis that defines and shapes successful performance improvement efforts, and maps the critical steps for insuring that a performance improvement program will meet real business needs and objectives.

Paperback, 298 pages, 9/96 • ISBN 1-57675-001-9 CIP
Item no. 50019-176 $24.95

Hardcover, 7/94 • ISBN 1-881052-48-6 CIP • **Item no. 52486-176 $34.95**

Evaluating Training Programs
The Four Levels

Donald L. Kirkpatrick

A COMPREHENSIVE step-by-step guide to evaluating training programs—from the creator of the "Kirkpatrick Model," the most widely used approach for evaluating training programs in industry, business, government, and academic institutions.

Paperback, 250 pages, 1/96 • ISBN 1-881052-85-0
Item no. 52850-176 $24.95

Hardcover, 11/94 • ISBN 1-881052-49-4 CIP • **Item no. 52494-176 $32.95**

On-The-Level
Performance Communication That Works
New Edition

Patricia McLagan and Peter Krembs

*D*ESIGNED TO HELP managers and employees plan and execute more effective and less fearful communication, *On The Level* provides tips, action steps, and practical tools to help everyone in and around the workplace communicate "on-the-level."

Paperback, 140 pages, 8/95 • ISBN 1-881052-76-1 CIP
Item no. 52761-176 $19.95

Available at your favorite bookstore, or call (800) 929-2929

Structured On-the-Job Training

Unleashing Employee Expertise in the Workplace

Ronald Jacobs and Michael Jones

JACOBS AND JONES describe an approach to on-the-job training that combines the structure of off-site training with the inherent efficiency of training conducted in the actual job setting. They show how structured OJT helps employees bridge the gap between learning job information and actually using that information on the job. *Structured On-the-Job Training* provides step-by-step guidelines for designing and delivering effective training in the actual job setting.

Hardcover, 220 pages, 1/95 • ISBN 1-881052-20-6 CIP
Item no. 52206-176 $29.95

Performance Consulting

Moving Beyond Training

Dana Gaines Robinson and James C. Robinson

PERFORMANCE CONSULTING provides a conceptual framework and many how-to's for moving from the role of a traditional trainer to that of a performance consultant. Dozens of useful tools, illustrative exercises, and a case study that threads through the book show how the techniques described are applied in an organizational setting.

Paperback, 320 pages, 1/96 • ISBN 1-881052-84-2 CIP
Item no. 52842-176 $24.95

Hardcover, 4/95 • ISBN 1-881052-30-3 CIP • **Item no. 52303-176 $34.95**

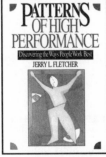

Patterns of High Performance

Discovering the Ways People Work Best

Jerry L. Fletcher

DISCOVERING your individual High Performance Pattern—the distinctive sequence of steps you naturally follow when you are at your best—is the key to energized performance, heightened creativity, and consistent excellence. Jerry Fletcher shows how to discover your High Performance Pattern to sustain outstanding results in a variety of complex, real-life situations.

Paperback, 270 pages, 2/95 • ISBN 1-881052-70-2 CIP
Item no. 52702-176 $17.95

Hardcover, 9/93 • ISBN 1-881052-33-8 CIP • **Item no. 52338-176 $27.95**

Available at your favorite bookstore, or call (800) 929-2929

A Higher Standard of Leadership
Lessons from the Life of Gandhi

Keshavan Nair

THIS IS THE FIRST BOOK to apply lessons from Gandhi's life to the practical tasks faced by today's business and political leaders. Through illustrative examples from Gandhi's life and writings, Keshavan Nair explores the process of making decisions, setting goals, and implementing actions in the spirit of service that is essential to the realization of a higher standard of leadership in our workplaces and communities.

Paperback, 174 pages, 1/97 • ISBN 1-57675-011-6 CIP
Item no. 50116-176 $16.95

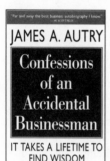

Confessions of an Accidental Businessman
It Takes a Lifetime to Find Wisdom

James A. Autry

IN *CONFESSIONS OF AN ACCIDENTAL BUSINESSMAN*, best-selling author James Autry blends candid and engaging autobiography with practical and realistic lessons in management and leadership. More than a memoir, it is a teaching tale for managers who seek to integrate their values in the creation of innovative, productive, and profitable organizations. Reflecting on his thirty-two years in business, Autry shares a lifetime of hard-earned wisdom about the art of business leadership, as well as the art of living a balanced life.

Hardcover, 250 pages, 10/96 • ISBN 1-57675-003 CIP
Item no. 75003-176 $24.95

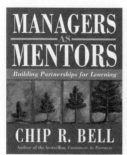

Managers As Mentors
Building Partnerships for Learning

Chip R. Bell

MANAGERS AS MENTORS is a provocative guide to helping associates grow and adapt in today's tumultuous organizations. Chip Bell's hands-on, down-to-earth advice takes the mystery out of effective mentoring, teaching leaders to be the confident coaches integral to learning organizations.

Hardcover, 200 pages, 6/96 • ISBN 1-881052-92-3 CIP
Item no. 52923-176 $24.95

Available at your favorite bookstore, or call (800) 929-2929